MORE DAK DICTA

MORE DAK DICTA

VERSES WRITTEN IN CALCUTTA
(1894-1910)

WILMOT CORFIELD

GYAN

Published by

Gyan Publishing House
5, Ansari Road
Daryaganj, New Delhi-110002
Phone: 011-47034999, 9811692060
E-mail: books@gyanbooks.com

Distribution Network
gyanbooks.com
India, USA, Canada, UK, Australia

ISBN: 978-93-7169-079-9 (PB)

First Published, 1911

2nd Impression 2025

Printed at: Gyan Press, Delhi.

MORE DAK DICTA
Author: WILMOT CORFIELD

Yours sincerely
Dâk

MORE DÂK DICTA

VERSES WRITTEN IN CALCUTTA

(1894—1910)

AND

PHILATELIC VERSES

BY

WILMOT CORFIELD, F.R.P.S.L., F.N.B.A., A.S.A.A

Member of the Royal Society of Arts

First Honorary Treasurer of the Calcutta Historical Society

Vice-President of the Philatelic Society of India; and of the Fiscal Philatelic Society (London)

SECOND EDITION

CALCUTTA

THACKER, SPINK AND CO

1911

TO MY WIFE

PREFACE.

My "Dâk Dicta" having been well received I now have pleasure in issuing the remainder of the verses written in Calcutta above my *nom-de-plume* "Dâk," with the same acknowledgments to previous publishers.

Some of my friends have expressed to me surprise that in the course of an exceptionally busy life I have found time for dalliance with one of the Muses. Perhaps they and others similarly astonished may find in the following extract from a London newspaper of a few weeks ago food for reflection of a kind to lighten their mental darkness; in some cases oh how great that darkness.

"In opening the winter session of the University College Hospital Medical School the Dean of Salisbury warned doctors against cultivating a too severely scientific habit of mind.

"The Dean said that if he were a director of a medical school he would advise the students that the realm of fine arts was that into which they should make excursions for the refreshment and enlargement of the mental life. In his judgment the most efficacious, as well as the most easily accessible hobby to counteract the influence of mental concentration on specialism was poetry, the queen of the arts.

"Let those who are piling up fees and rushing from one thing to another on to a baronetcy—(laughter)—stop their motor-car when they pass the National Gallery and enter and gaze for a minute or two at the Madonna of the Rocks, or go to the British Museum and seek the great statues of Theseus or Dionysius. 'But poetry you can have with you every day,' added the Dean, amid applause."

And to the good Dean's closing remark may I further add "and also verse?"

W. C.

CALCUTTA,
19th December, 1910.

CONTENTS.

CONTENTS.

CONTENTS.

PART II.

RUPERT'S RAID.

(*3rd April* 1643.)

FLING wide the pane—I hear them call—
  The bells are calling, clear and free,
Come closer, children, one and all,
  And you, my blue-eyed Dorothy,
Creep closest, dearest, press my cheek—
The bells are there, I hear them speak.

Oh, God! they call as called they then:
  (Toss back the curtain from my bed)
I mind the tread of marching men!
  I mind the torches' burning dread!—
How those wild bells went hurtling wide
From Harborne's brow that Eastertide.

For Rupert came, with steel and flame;
  And all the world with war went red;—
From Bourne to Rea, from Rea to Tame,
  The reeking ravens shrieking sped;—
And all the while from Harborne's brow
The bells rang out—they're ringing now.

Some strove, they say, for Church and King;—
  (God saw and shrank to stay the wrong)
And some for lust of fight,—they ring
  The bells go ringing all day long.
And most for home, and child, and wife,
  For England's laws and England's life.

The town within the hollow there
  Was all alive the foe to smite;
There hammered anvils rent the air,
  And forges flared by day and night.
The ford was flanked by wagons piled,
The bridge-way fenced—(come closer, child!)

My son (your uncle, children mine;
  A goodlier son ne'er woman bare)
In buff and scarlet garb shewed fine,
  Astride Grey Bess, our dappled mare,
As spurring to my cottage side,
"Christ save us, mother!" thus he cried.

"King Charles' force make Lichfield Fane
  With drake and sacre. Horse and man,
Twelve hundred strong are under rein,
  And ruthless Rupert heads their van
In haste to pay us back our call
On Thomas Holte at Aston Hall!"

"The Prince will reach the town to-day,
  They drub the drums on yonder green,
Our musters thicken for the fray
  And blades are set and pikes are keen;
'For God and Right,' the people shout!"
("For God and Right," the bells rang out.)

I kissed him there before the men;
  I watched them wend down Harborne Hill,
Into the vale they dipped, and then
  They crossed the Chad's reed-woven rill—
I see them, see them now, although
'Twas three score years save five ago.

I strained to catch the last faint glow
  Of light from off his corslet cast,
The wan, wild sun scarce served to show
  Each glinting plume as on they passed—
A sturdy warrior cavalcade—
To bear the brunt of Rupert's raid.

A brook was by, I laved my head,
  And gat me home, and sought to sleep;
Above the town the sky lowered red,
  We women watched but could not weep—
And through the street and down the hill
The men went townward, townward still.

All night yon church tower reeling hurled
  A clamorous tocsin near and far;
All night the battle-clangour whirled,
  And great fires blazed on Clent and Barr.
And some saw sights not good to tell;
May Mary shrive their souls from hell!

A cloud-fiend, with a brazen brand,
  Fled yammering with a muffled face—
From Cofton Firs his pinions spanned
  And merged in mist on Sutton Chase,—
A murky monster, maundering wrath,
Great spume spates flecking all his path.

He passed, and round the welkin's rim
  Fell shapes belaboured each in strife;
Unhallowed jargon, strange and grim,
  Jangled the air with discord rife—
(So gossips tell) as sobs and knells
Were flung from Harborne's throbbing bells.

A spectre hand with shadowy axe
  Loomed large aslant of Tennel Hall,
Pale formless hounds in phantom packs
  Thrice skirted Quinton's churchyard wall,
And slabs were seen to heave and sway
O'er grey escutcheoned vaults, men say.

Yes, turn my pillow, lay it so,
  And place some water to my lip,
All these things happed long years ago,
  When yon great elm was but a slip.
How sweet that bright laburnum smells!
God saw it all—there go the bells!

Next day, at dawn, I hied to town;
  At noon the trumpet charge rang loud,
And Rupert's horsemen sweeping down,
  Crashed, cursing, through our feeble crowd.
I saw them tear through Digbeth mire
As fiends aflush with hell's own fire

Boots it to tell? You know the tale!
  The steel-shod stallions forward strode,
With thrust and stab and stroke as flail
  Resistless Rupert onward rode;
Then stalled his steed in Martin's porch
And gave the town to loot and torch.

My son! My son! I sought him long,
  Where dead lay thick, where lust ran high,
Where ribald roysterers wrought them wrong,
  'Twere pain to speak. The star-pierced sky
Stretched one vast shame-fed shrieking pall
From Stratford Grange to Leather Hall.

The stench from Master Porter's dam,
  Where dead in slime lay festering, they
Who'd fallen fronting Rupert's ram
  That forced the mill, filled every way
With fever-freighted puffs, rolled thick
Till strong men reeled to feel its lick.

The Anchor, where the Prince caroused,
  The Crown-house, where red Rhenish flowed,
The Cross, where bated bears are housed
  And bulls are spiked for sport, each showed
An aftermath of beastial fight
In Bromwicham that fiery night.

I sought my boy and sought him wide,
  I searched through good King Edward's Guild
Where frightened women crouched and cried
  (The ample Court with troopers filled),
With smoke-veiled eyes and grief-split heart,
The lamb-house and the Goddes Cart.

The Chepe aflame with beasts was loud
  Broke loose from out the shambles near—
Horned beasts, hides roasting, hacked and houghed,
  Thronged raging, bellowing, steer to steer—
Pert drink-stuffed hoydens haggling by
To see the grand brutes screeching die.

There, shift my shoulders, let me look
  On glebe all green and church half rust,
Where Parson Ward from gold rimmed book
  On Sundays tell us "God is just."
It must be so—to doubt is sin—
Though great bulls burn while wantons grin.

No sparrow falls, no swallow fails,
  He knows it well, and He is good;
But babes were ripped on park-fence rails
  That night hard by in Ladywood,
And girls were thrust to worse than death,
"The Lord is love" so parson saith.

No more, no more, of that cruel past
  Of havoc-wreck and endless ache—
The bells are flying, plying fast—
  (Good lack, my hands are all ashake!)
Dead, dead, I looked my last on him
Beneath the lych-gate's yew-shade dim.

I'd staggered home, scarce knowing why,
  Old Tib mewed moping by the door.
The ash-strewn grey cold hearth, anigh
  Was Don stretched snoring on the floor,
When clear across the sprouting corn,
The drone of muffled drums was borne.

'Twas he they bore with martial tread
  And earth-cast look and halting stride,
For him, the dead, the glorious dead,
  They stirred the turf that Eastertide ;
The passing bell boomed forth elate
To greet him 'neath the ledged lych-gate.

The first to buffet Rupert's swoop,
  'Twas he hurled Denby from his cell ;
He hewed a track through Digby's troop,
  And lopped and lashed the charge to quell ,
Five foemen harried him in vain
Through Walmore Fields and Congrees Lane.

Leech Tillam, standing at his door,
  Was shot to death. He cleft the cur
Who snapt the cock from cheek to jaw ;
  Then, sword unwiped and dripping spur,
Dashed on to succour Greaves' band
Who battled Digby hand to hand.

And Digby fell at Good Knave's End,
  And graceless Denby bit the gorse
At Shirland bounds—(may Christ forfend
  The sin-wage of his rueful course !)
And he, my son, wound-faint, athirst,
Swooned, death-smote by the Ravenhurst.

In wooded haunt, where ravens brood,
  On bracken couched, at vesper tide
He slid to sleep in solitude,
  The bells, the bells still floating wide,—
The bells from grey-towered Harborne's brow,
St. Peter's bells—they're ringing now.

The axe smote straight at Whitehall gate;
Grim Oliver in storm hath sped;
An alien heir shapes England's fate,
And England honours England's dead,—
The bells ring on,—and ne'er shall fade
The stern, sad tale of Rupert's raid.

"*Edgbastonia.*" (*Birmingham*) *August* 1894.

SHELVED.

(**The Calcutta Improvement Scheme.*)

"Unhappily, Lord Curzon's services are not available and we must wait till somebody else turns up." Wilmot Corfield in the "Empire," 26th October, 1906.

'TIS well to preach and 'tis well to prate and 'tis well to be slinging the *gup*,
But better to leave the righting of wrong till somebody else turns up.
Ho! bring me stylos and flagons of ink with blue-lined reams of the best,
And never forget the safe old saw "the land hath need of a rest."

The town hath need of a big new broom—a broom of the goodliest brand—
A broom that will rush through slime and slush when somebody comes to hand,
The town hath Death on the dance-a-shout, from the core to the border's rim,
So we sleep, let the fleshless fool fling on—why worry a bit about him?

Ah me! when the man with the mind comes by, when that somebody else is found,
How the slime will slink and the spectre fly and the spade and the pick resound.
How the great good sun and the reeking earth will grapple it hot and strong.
Ho! the pest will pass and the plague will die when somebody comes along.

---

* *In a speech by Lord Curzon towards the end of his first period of office he is reported to have said that were he not Viceroy he would like to be Chairman of the Calcutta Corporation with a free hand.*

"The land hath need of a rest," they say, but the town of a broom, and so
When that somebody somewhere comes this way we don't for the moment know.
The smoke curls white from the *ghât's* hot lip, and the death gongs rattle apace,
And the people are pent in a palsied grip at the heel of an alien race.

We hold the land as "a trust for aye," and the town rots under a pall,
But the land needs rest, and the people die and nobody's coming at all.
The flag of the English King flaunts wide to the haze of a brazen sky,
And the white flares red where the flame leaps light but nobody else comes by.

Then bring me stylos and bring me ink and blue-lined reams of the best—
The *hukhum* hath come from the Talking-house where the white men rule in the west
And the neck and the crop of the Why? is this—that the land hath need of a rest—

So look to it well that ye sleep apace and snore as the death-gongs ring,
While the *tom-toms* beat in a frenzied chase to the laud of the spectre king,
And heed ye well as ye drain the dregs of the "rest-cure's" somnolent cup
Don't ever tackle a wrong but wait till somebody else turns up.

The Empire, 30th October 1906.

OUT OF PATIENCE.

(A REJOINDER.)

"In spite of the gibe of our poetic contributor, 'Dak,' the general feeling was that the land *had* need of a rest......... Lord Minto came to India and he has gone on from strength to strength. He has not made as many speeches in twelve months as some Viceroys would already have made in the course of the Cold weather tour ....Lord Minto is to be most respectfully congratulated upon his brilliant silences."—The *Empire*, 24th November 1906.

"The jokes of even our new, and ably conducted, evening newspaper are not always readily apparent." –Mr. S. K. Ratcliffe in the course of "An Evening with Punch" at the Y. M. C. A., 24th November 1906.

IF you're anxious to define the correct Viceregal line
And dilute it down to merely *laissez faire* —
You dilate in glowing phrase
On these simple silent days
And you please folks everywhere.
You must pose as an apostle
Of an age that doesn't jostle
On a non-committal pacifying plan—
Dhurrumtollah and Chowringhee
And each motor, tram and *dinghy*
Will proclaim "There—that's the man!"
And everyone will say, etc.

You musn't sound the praise of the spacious Curzon days
That have long since known decay,
But sing out we've one at length
Who goes on from strength to strength
In a placid, pleasing, passive sort of way.
Send the pæan on in printo
By a *peon* to Lord Minto—
Who'll say "thank you, very kindly, Mr. Blair;"
And don't listen to the gibe
Of a versifying scribe
Who had scented Retrogression in the air.
And everyone will say
(As the "Empire" carves its way)
"That 'Empire' man expresses himself in terms that just suit me;
"Why what a most imperially minded man
"That 'Empire' man must be!"

The Empire, 26th November 1906.

HORRIBILE BILLI.

Or the Billi that Dikhed you :

(An old saw re-set.)

" A correspondent writes to us complaining of the nuisance occasioned by the prevalence of stray dogs in the neighbourhood of Gurranhatta. We are astonished that no one has yet written about the cats in the neighbourhood of Chowringhee."—The " EMPIRE, " 13th December 1906.

GRUDGE not the *billi jat*
  Infant immersion—
Tabby or " torture " shell,
  Mongrel or Persian—
Whate'er the prowler's name,
All cats are just the same,
All play the same old game—
  Direful diversion.
Brick-bats, etc.

Where'er the *billi* prowls
  People cry " drat her !"
Chowringhee, Ballyganj
  Or Gurranhatta.
Calcutta night by night
Writhes while the felines fight ;
Spar, spoon and spit and smite,
  Chortle and chatter
Brick-bats, etc.

" Calcutta Day by Day "
  Dreads her excursions,
  While the S. P. C. A.
  Sighs its aversions.
  Daylight and dark attest
  Pussy's a perfect pest.
  Wipe her out, paw to crest,
  Spite her " purr " versions.
  Brick-bats, etc.

Daylight and dark attest
  Pussy's aspersions.
How can the sleeper rest
  'Till each one her shuns ?

End all her mewling pranks—
Torture shell, Tom or Manx,
And earn our lasting thanks
By prompt immersions.
Brick-bats! Brick-bats!
Of what avail are they
By night or day
For those marauding cats?
Brick-bats!

The Empire, 15th December, 1906.

THE TALE OF A TOWN HALL.

List to the latest untwistable tale,
All about nothing at all,
Told of our moribund, obsolete, stale,
Jocular old Town-hall,
Low has it laughed as it lingers along—
When we're all dead 'twill be still going strong.

THE Minto Fête was ended, and we hadn't much to do,
While our village green reverted to its customary hue;
And the papers lacked a topic to enthrill a jaded town,
For we'd gone up like a rocket and we felt the coming down.

Now the planetary systems that go twirling round in space
Have a whimsical affection for a jaded human race,—
So the planetary systems cogitated on a plan
To evolve for our convenience both the moment and the man.

The moment was propitious for it happened at a point
When we went about remarking that the times were out of joint,
While we failed to catch the humour scintillating from the swag
That they told us emanated from a pushful "lucky-bag."

The man too was propitious, which his name was Mr. Phelps;
He'd a project most ambitious, knowing every little helps,
And he set to work with vigour making all of us believe
Him a coruscating comet with a town-hall up his sleeve.

And he told us, yes he told us, at the Hall Y. M. C. A.
(With his thumb inserted neatly in his waistcoat, by the way,)
That our town-hall acted shocking tugging at the civic purse
And whenever we improved it, why we only made it worse.

I cannot quite remember all the desolating stacks
Of disclosures disconcerting that he reckoned up in *lakhs*
To a mental memorandum on the mischief that was made
When they placed that pillared chamber on the Western Esplanade.

Then someone went and grappled with a weirdly wild machine
And the flickering town-halls wobbled upside down across the screen,
Thus we all of us experienced a too enchanting while,
And detested sister cities who could do the thing in style.

Till, at last, we struck a vision of a *bustee* coarse and crude,
Then the speaker with elation struck a proper attitude
And observed with pride parental as he pointed " there you are,
There's the site to build a town-hall,—which its in the Jaun Bazar."

We tried, but couldn't see it, though it may smell just as sweet
Transmogrified from " Jaun Bazar " to " Corporation Street "—
And remorse retained its victims when we passed a vote of thanks—
For again we knew the feeling that comes on when drawing blanks.

With an air of stern decision that he nearly always wears
At about the hour of mid-night when the're burglars on the stairs,
Mr. Allen then proceeded to enunciate the creed
That a proper civic spirit must precede the civic deed.

We are watching for that spirit, we are glancing up and down,
Just to catch the inspiration of its presence in the town,
It's a fascinating spirit and we wish 'twould come our way,—
Like the elephant that sauntered gently in on K. of K.

That the planetary systems all awhirling round about
Are still working to beguile us there is not the slightest doubt,
For at the next assemblage of the Council, so they say,
Mr. Phelps proposed a motion to donate the Hall away.

We had settled down to ponder on his sacrificing plan—
But the clock that struck the moment also closured out the man—
For the planetary systems have a complicated trick
Of slapping an extinguisher on mortal methods—slick.

So we waited the *daynoomong* till the meeting yesterday
But Mr. Phelps, if present, didn't give the Hall away,
A pound of tea costs money when you haven't got the tin,
And who would take the Town-hall without the tea thrown in ?

There are morals lurking somewhere in this unimposing *gup*.—
Mr. Phelps will ne'er be Viceroy for he likes to wake us up—
Never cultivate the habit of donating Halls away.—
Don't wait till six is striking to say what you have to say.—

Never head a public movement—but catch burglars when you can,—
And always miss the moment while you overlook the man :—
And never, never, never fan the civic spirit's flame—
Leave the job to those who like it—and you'll get there all the same.

The Empire, 14th March 1907.

JOB CHARNOCK'S PROPHETIC SOLILOQUY.

From a fragment which ought to have been picked up near a marble slab on a club* gate-post in Chowringhee :—

HAIL to the last asylum !
  Hail to the wanderer's haven !
Hail to the rents that rise sky-high
  And the path that's still unpaven—
Here hard by Boytaconnah,
  Under Sealdah's height,
All in the land of *Materam*—
  Is fixed the glorious site.

Hurrah ! for the great city
  That stretches many a mile—
Hurrah for gallant merchant-men
  Who passing make their pile :—
Thine, Briton, is the *pilum*,
  Briton the pile is thine,
The ordered line of stock and share—
  The corn and oil and wine.

There, where the leopard ranges
  On Howrah's further shore
The flare from endless flues shall rise
  For endless looms that roar ;—
And here by miles of jetties
  Some day the dust shall foam
'Fore the bright eyes of wives and girls
  Whose berths are booked for home.

***The old Bengal Club, since demolished.**

All hail ! to Clive's stout *pilum*,
All hail ! the Income-tax,
All hail ! the chain of worth that winds
From Madame Grand to " Max" ;—
Now by the scented Maidan
The motor-bus is seen—
And clubs and pubs where tiger-cubs
Make frolic on the green.

Blest, and thrice blest, the Briton
Who sees Ind's proudest day—
Who sees this big malodorous swamp
Start on its wondrous way—
Here, 'neath this spreading *peepul*,
Bid me the future probe
That booms the everlasting fame
Of Capitalian Job.

Bengal : Past and Present, October, 1907.

THE LION (Not to mention the Unicorn).

A fragment of " for Cotton Lore. "

* "*Particularly noticeable on the east and west (of Government House) are the four fine gateways, surmounted by the figure of a lion.*"

YOU know, of course, that pile sublime
Where floats a flag at Christmas time—
With sentries marching in and out
While scarlet *peons* walk about ;—
Its where we go, quite free from cares,
To *levées* and the like affairs.

I've been and bought a volume rare
From Mr. Eden in the Square ;
You've only got to give a look
To find it a delightful book :
(I quote the passage that I love
In neat italics up above).

Our paw was placed all *comme il faut* near F. H. Hathaway & Co.
The next one rested on the gate *en face* (that's French) to Diamond Tait
And one right on the other side topped the third gate (prodigious stride !),
The last was on the gate to hand where Steuart Bayley used to stand.

* From Calcutta Old and New by Mr. H. E. A. Cotton. The Lion on Government House must have faced either east or west.

The figure towered when quite at home
High o'er the flag-staff on the dome—
(The sort of brute to keep your eye on
And something like a British Lion).

The Unicorn, if built to scale,
Is not referred to in the tale,
Perhaps he found snug quarters near
Astride the top of Belvedere.
(Oh, what a fine titanic fight
When *they* commenced to snarl and bite !).

Dear Mr. Cotton, H. E. A.
I'm sorry, Sir, you've gone away—
You might have let your stylo flow
On that colossal beast, you know ;
If this perchance your eye should hit—
Do tell us what became of it.

(" One gate, one Paw " was, so they say,
The measure of an elder day—
But, *pace* Mr. Cotton's try on,—
The rule is now "One gate, one Lion.")

Bengal : Past and Present, October, 1907.

---

* THE VOICE OF THE VENGEANCE.

THE Vengeance came down like a wolf on the fold
Where the engines were gleaming in varnish and gold,
And the reek of its wrath raged from near and from far
When it held up the might of the great E. I. R.

With the strength of a Titan, secure and serene,
That line with its legions at sunset was seen,
Like a field that is fallow when harvest is mown
That strength on the morrow lay withered and strewn.

For the voice of the Vengeance grew great on the blast,
And it called to the man in the cab as he passed,
And the heart of the engine waxed deadly and chill
And its crank gave one turn and was silent and still.

---

* A formidable strike of drivers and others was in progress on the East Indian Railway.

For gone was the speed of the piston aslide,
Behind it there hissed not the steam of its stride,
And the flare of the furnace flamed red on the rail
Where it flashed out a halt to the on-coming mail.

And there sat the driver, excited and warm,
With the sweat on his brow and the dust on his arm,
The signals all useless, the coolies all flown,
The luggage unlifted, the whistle unblown.

And the place that is Fairlie is loud in its wail
For the chances are broke for the big Punjab mail,
And the might that is motion on gauge that is broad
Is melted like snow on the Main and the Chord.

The Empire, 23rd November, 1907.

UNHISTORIC CALCUTTA.

(Quite unreliable.)

"ONE GATE, ONE SLAB."

"A somewhat belated copy of "Bengal : Past and Present" has reached us, but it is well worth waiting for ; our only grievance against it is that it seems to have carried off our contributor "Dâk." We experience a certain feeling of relief on hearing from him again as we were thinking of advertising. It is impossible not to admire the keenness of the Calcutta Historical Society. It simply bubbles with antiquarian zeal."—*The Empire.*

"ONE man, One vote !" they used to say
In my receding boyhood's day,
But now those with the gift of gab
Ejaculate "One gate, One slab !"

Go buy, there is no need to wait
(The price *pro tem :* is just two eight)
Our "Was and Is" our "B : P. P."
(Two nickels more per V. P. P.)

There was a city, fair and wide,
Inclined a bit to put on side,
For she was blessed by kindly fate
With many a most imposing gate.

While some were arched, and some were brick
And some were tall and others thick
The passers by on 'bus or tram
Observed that most were buff *chunam.*

There was a Viceroy, proud and prim,
And it was his peculiar whim
To find a gate and then to dab
Upon that gate a marble slab.

The habit grew as habits do,
And grew, and grew, and grew, and grew.
He'd rise up early, sit up late,
To go and decorate a gate.

He also had a pleasing plan
To place a Hall on the Maidan,
He placed it here, he placed it there.
(Just now its somewhere in the air.)

He labelled with emphatic grace
Each pretty statue's granite base.
Such things to him, or small or great
Were each profound Affairs of State.

Until at last there came the day
When o'er the seas he sailed away,
And some, when he was lost to view,
Cried "Whaur's Nathaniel ganged the noo?"

All these were they who liked a gate
Best unadorned, in nature's state.
(I quite decline to take their cue
And don't accept their point of view.)

But other folk, the more refined,
Had feelings of less crude a kind,
And these with bubbling zeal cried "stop,—
His mantle's tumbled on us, flop!"

We will not leave to luckless fate
A single solitary gate,
We will not sing, nor laugh, nor dance
Till every slab has had its chance.

While our lost leader sounds the call
For "Oxford," "Clive" and "Crosby Hall,"
Let our exultant war-cry ring
"Darwaza hai"—"the gate's the thing!"

See where his dust dimmed banners rest,
Lo, on the wall his lance and crest,
Why should these war-worn emblems rot?
Go take them down and use the lot!

Out Firminger with " B: P. P.!"
Up Huddleston and Rampini!
Ho " Max " and Madge, a fray, a fray—
Cry " Dunbar " and a " J. de Grey!"

We mean to see this business through
And do the thing in style, we do.
And that's the reason, more or less
Of our resounding C. H. S.

* * * *

I'm very glad, A. J. F. B.,
To find you've not forgotten me.
I rather like your neat remark,
Accept this verse and keep it

DAK.

The Empire, 28th November, 1907.

CONCILIATION

OR SHPOILIN' TH' STROUBLE.

(With apologies to the shade of " Ingoldsby.")

OCH! Conciliation! what termination
To arl th' bhotheration can wid ut compare?
When Mist'r Engelken wid arl th' Union men
Likewise th' Agint for a sittlemint did prepare.
'Tis, now you'll see th' Thraffic Manager
Shpoilin' th' panic—allanah an' asthore!—
An' *sahibs* an' Committees wid hunks iv tied up *chitties*
Arl shtandin' round before th' chamber door.

Th' platforms lavin', ne'er a wan a gravin',
Lost time retravin', down from Assansol;—
Wid patter an' palavar like sparrers made in Java
Arl wishful to shtruggle up out iv a big hole.
Now there approaches five dozen coaches—
'Mid gineral clamour,—och! 'twas mighty foine
To see how aisy—nippy as a daisy—
Arl thim rogues iv ingines came galumphin' down th' line.

Back to Howrah's charums after th' alarums,
Picknickin' in spayshuls, carriages first class,
Open go th' chamber gates to th' bould delegates—
Iviry shplendid foightin' bhoy turnin' up *ong masse.*
First to Kellner's arl retratin' for an uninformal matin'
"Bhoys, here's th' Agint'—sing a horotorio—
An' if an owdacious thraitor on infarior orator
Puts on frills at that sure I'd like to tell him so."

There's Mist'r Allen walkin', like a Lord Mayor, talkin'
To Dumayne an' Monteath, haroes iv renown;
An' gyards an' ingine dhrivers an' tillygraft arrivers
Purradin' in owld Clive Estreet, back agin in town.
Thimsilves presadin', Mist'r Dhring a ladin',
The blessed Saints could tell us, who into th' chair,—
An' that foine fellow—fresh an' free an' mellow—
Darlint Mist'r Huddleston, th' *chargy-defair.*

Sure, uts thim what rises airly *dong le place de la Fairlie,*
Where th' railway rulers meet to cogitate,
An' sure uts Mist'r Dhring who has had us arl on shtring,
Faix an' uts himself we arl shud emulate.
Mist'r "Max" th' burly—A. D. C. to Shirley—
In th' press gallery you might persave,
But Engleken was missin', chanst he'd gone a fishin'
After other gintlemin had koindly given lave.

See th' porters, an' th' sorters, an' th' newspaper reporters,
(Th' "Journal" man a snippin' iv pincils by th' score);—
Och! I'll be bhothered an' entoirly shmothered
To tell wan half of thim as was to th' fore.
Wid our Corporation (salt iv arl th' nation),
The Port Commission, an' th' Y. M. C. A.
But th' European-Anglo-Defence-Assofandango
Knew ut wasn't whanted, so ut shtay'd away.

Mast'r Dhring (Saints bless him) och! they did address him;
Foine an' mighty monarch, nuthin' left to learn,
Like Cæsar, great Agrippa, or Rooseveldt th' skipper,
Napowleon, th' O'Cromwell, or Mist'r S. Thremearne.
Thin there was shoutin' an' a good store in spoutin'
(For its mysilf was sittin' forninst th' quality)
An' Mist'r Dhring said "thank ye for arl this hanky panky,
*Its a toidy toime a comin'—I mean that C. I. E."

---

* Happily it has since arrived.

Then the Foort salooted, an' arl th' conferince scooted,
Cryin' "Heavin save King Edward an' our Royal Dhring!"
Och! an its mysilf shud live to be a hundrid
Sure an its th' proudest day I'll iver sing.
Faix now I've inded fwhat I've invinted,
This mendacious narrative, widoubt fear or fuss,
Shtrikin' dhrys th' throttle, pass along th' bottle,
Faith, its mysilf—Och! *toro bhurruf—bus!*

The Journal, 22nd December, 1907.

THE IMPASSE AND THE ELEPHANT.

(The opponents of the Victoria Memorial Hall Scheme now contend on the eve of defeat that the White Elephant has arrived at an Impasse.)

THE Impasse and the Elephant
Were sobbing hand in hand;
They sighed like anything to see
Their backers undermanned:
If Curzon's Scheme were cleared away'
They said, 'it would be grand!'

'O Experts, say a word for us!'
—The Impasse did implore—
'Make out the pile will sink a mile
And buckle, roof and floor,—
We cannot do with more than three—
The fees don't run to more.'

Then three fine experts hurried up
The Scheme to shake or make,
They talked of strain and stress and truss,
Of tie-bar, block, and break.
The Elephant said 'thank you, but
You've made my fore-head ache.'

'The time has come,' the Impasse said,
'To talk of many things:
Of Leveés, Balls, and Belvedere'—
'The season always brings
A pleasant change,' the Hathi said,
'To Engelkens and Drings!'

'But wait a bit', the Experts cried,
'Before we have our chat—
The three of us are of a mind—
Now, what d'you think of that?
We cannot go and sink the show;
So there you have it pat!'

'If mighty "Max" wrote "Current Coin"
A million years of grace,
Do you suppose,' the Impasse said,
'He'd engineer our case?'
'I doubt it,' said the Elephant,
And mopped his pallid face.

'Those lovely texts that "Max" evolves
Are soothing to the soul',—
'They're fine,' remarked the Impasse, 'but
'I wish he'd stick to Coal!
'Or Jute,' observed the Elephant,
'My friend—we're in a hole!'

'Don't mention "Max",' the Impasse said,
'I'm feeling out of sorts;
The air is thick, it makes me sick,
With expertised Reports,—
B. P. and G. have done for me,
And now we've E's retorts!'

'Just so! just so!' the other said,
'You look a little cheap!
This talk of "Max" and wasted lakhs
Has set me all a-creep!'
Then some-one called out 'Birdcage!' and
They tumbled in a heap.

'Poor, funny things,' Lord Minto smiled
When passing, so they say,
'Won't some one bring an ambulance
To cart the pair away?
And now for Marble, Bricks and Work,—
They've had their little day!

The Journal, *12th January*, 1908.

"BONNIE DUNDEE."

(An old song re-set.)

Mr. Winston Churchill, speaking at the Reform Club, Manchester, said his defeat was a heavy blow and the consequences would be grave and serious. It is understood that the Liberals of Dundee have telegraphed asking him to contest Dundee."

TO the Manchester merchants 't was Churchill who spoke—
"Ma chances are doon, I'm a little bit broke—
So let each volunteer who loves Asquith and me—
Cry 'Aye !' to the offer frae Bonnie Dundee !
Come pack up ma' baggage, come pick up ma' sticks,
Come book for the Border and 'goodbye' to Hicks.
I'll hook it for Scotland and come back M. P.—
Oh its hey for the Border and Bonnie Dundee !"

Now see him dismounted, cock sure in defeat,—
Though his bills are unbacked and his party all beat,—
" They chucked Balfour (douce mon)" says he so let it be—
We're well rid o' this toon—hech for Bonnie Dundee.
So mak' for the station as quick as you can—
Tak' saxpence and wire to Dundee 'I'm your man,'
For Asquith, Burns, Birrell, and little Lloyd, G.
Have not yet seen the last of their Winston (that's ME).

There are streams beyond Irwell and votes beyond Forth,—
There is cotton doon south, but there's whisky up north,
Dinna fash yoursel', England, ye'll no have to wait,
For this chiel will improve on that 4988.
Then toss the portmanteaus and traps in the van,
Macwinston Machurchill's your 'sponsible man,
Ma 'jiggin's unsettled, but e'en let it be—
For I ken on'y step they may ca' in Dundee !"

The Empire, April, 1908.

WAKING IT UP (Part I).

"The Council of the European Defence Association met in strength yesterday afternoon to discuss a number of questions of no little importance to the European community, which it would not be prudent to publish at the moment. The members present were Mr. Lockbart Smith, Vice-President, Messrs. W. L. Simmons, and W. Smith, Vice-President, Mr. B. L. Williams, Honorary Treasurer, and Messrs. F. Burns, A. G. Prestow, B. H. A. Gresson, J. B. Straws, F. A. Talmony, W. A. Duncan, H. D. Wood, A. Taffing, H. W. S. Sparkes. It would be different to form a meeting of more largely and influentially representative men, and it may be assumed that this meeting would be as interesting as any could well be at this time."—(Literal transcription from the '*Englishman*,' 30th June, 1908.)

GO tell the tale to town and tide—
  Its waking up at length,—
The E. D. A. is yawning wide
  And going to go in strength.
And when you've told the glorious '*gup*'
  Go tell it all again,—
For Smith's no myth, the Sparkes fly up,—
  In classic Mangoe Lane.

But things are passing strange indeed—
  The times are odd to-day
When Englishmen of English breed
  Direct the E. D. A.
Who, lest the hurtling bomb should boom
  And end their patriot game,
Sit round about the Council room
  In some-one-else's name.

The President, as Lockbart hight,
  Made the proceedings go—
Sir Lock Smith, Bart., (no common knight)
  Would sound more '*apropos.*'
Can Simmons, L., be Simmons, J.
  Our old and trusted friend ?
That Smith is "on" is good, but pray
  Where will his caperings end ?

Does B. L. Williams hide the head of R. L. Williamson ?—
  Did Mister Prestow come instead of him yclept Preston?—
Did Gresson drop his R and gain by substituting B—
  While J. B. Straws for J. R. Strain looked on approvingly?
Topping as Taffing fearless tried
  One of his little larks,—
Though Duncan *Sahib* with proper pride
  Changed not, nor Wood nor Sparkes.

How did they to the meeting glide?
  How did they reach the place?
In cloak of black with stealthy stride
  And mask envisored face?

But none the less they meant to please—
  The '*Englishman*' is right,
It would be hard in times like these
  To meet a finer sight.
It would be 'different' to form
  A meeting so repre-
    sentative, or with hearts as warm
  For England, you and me.

WAKING IT UP.* (PART II.)

I fear I did the E. D. A.
  A lamentable wrong
In Tuesday's '*Empire*' (yesterday)
  About its going strong.
The consequences I can't shirk,
  I did, I did defame
In pointing out they went to work
  Each in a borrowed name.

To-day the '*Englishman*,' I find,
  Is rather rough on me,
And so I haste to ease my mind
  With this apology.
It lists to-day a different throng
  Of statesmen who were there,
And sets a new complexion on
  A half-and-half affair.

For thirteen climbed those endless stairs
  (A number dead to luck)
To regulate out state affairs
  And prove their patriot pluck.
And Hare Street hinted ten of them
  Flung down defensive gage
Disguised as common fameless men.
  (A weighty average).

* The *Englishman* shewed its appreciation by re-producing these verses in its own columns, and, on a writer calling himself "Balk" retaliating in verse, a newspaper controversy resulted.

And so good Harris never posed
As "Burns" and never shrank
By "Talmony" mis-diagnosed
As Larmour (was it Frank?)
O '*Englishman*', the old discreet
'The great, the good,' the ripe,—
O '*Englishman*' of March, Hare Street,
Look to your linotype.

The Empire, 30th June and 1st July, 1908.

ALL IN THE SAME SWIM.

BEFORE Bengal was cut at wish of potent Curzon
Our Mookerjee was but an unexacting person.
About his own affairs he was discreetly quiet
And never used the Squares for purposes of riot.

He ate his curry *bhat* and smoked his *hubble bubble*
And seldom took to heart a real or fancied trouble.
But when Bengal forsooth was slit by ruthless razor
He hinted things uncouth of good Sir Andrew Fraser.

A minced Bengal somehow confused his panorama :—
He engineered a row, and worked it,—tongs and hammer.
And whispered things out loud, and ran unhallowed presses,
And shocked the flawless crowd of sapient I. C. S.'s.—

He stood upon a chair and vididly orated,
And didn't cut his hair, and went and agitated.
He'd yearnings by the score and cardiac palpitations,
And Mr. "Max" said "lor! what lofty aspirations!"

The '*Statesman*' with regret indulged in wordy platitude,
Though the '*Exchange Gazette*' maintained a placid attitude.
The '*News*' blew hot and cold, but nothing in particular,
The '*Band Programme*' still sold to waiting folk vehicular.

The '*Englishman*' said "flam," the '*Empire*' heard and purred,
And '*Bande Mataram*' went nap on every word.
And so it came to hap a martyr has arisen—
For Mookerjee, poor chap, got carted off to prison.

And Great Ones in the Hills, all calm, and cool, and jolly
Called his eccentric frills "a passing phase of folly."
Cool heads are sometimes right, the wise one pre-supposes
They've made distinctly quite a proper diagnosis.

For Mookerjee will tire of his spasmodic rabies,
And soothe his patriot ire on succulent *jellabies*.
He'll turn quite good and nice, and stop his curious capers,
And cease to weigh out *pice* for fire and fury papers.

He's quite as fond of us, as we are fond of him—
So why this silly fuss? "We're all in the same swim!"
Though should he kick the trace,—of folly no forsaker—
Then it will be a case of "Pull d—l and pull Baker."

The Journal, 5th July, 1908.

RAMPINI'S OFF TO-DAY.

"Many crowded round to say good-bye to Sir Robert Fulton Rampini who finally retired last Thursday after forty-four years in the country. The following lines, composed on Howrah Station platform by that eminent versifier "Dâk," just before the mail left, very aptly sum up the general sentiments of regret which the retirement of so popular a personage everywhere inspired."—The *Journal.*

GOOD bye, Sir Robert! What so is is best—
A gallant course and now a famous rest,—
The rains are on and skies are leaden grey—
'Tis fitting so—for you are off to-day.

We'll miss you in the Courts when lost to sight,
Our law's chief lord, you kept its 'scutcheon white,—
We'll miss you on the lawn with glass to eye
What time the Apcar colours gallop by.

We'll miss you standing in your place at Paul's
When choir and clergy make the chancel stalls,—
And from the corner peals the organ sweet
While verger Hobson lots the unfilled seat,—

And from the stately Levée's kindly crowd
As, gloved, we brave the penned procession proud,
Till, Wellesley's hall of marble Cæsars past,
We scan the few who flank the throne at last.

We'll miss you while the "Jianti" tugs and strains
Above the bridge her harnessed mooring chains,
And pants for parts that always more or less
Yield learned copy for the C. H. S.

We'll miss you, now the hour has come to part;
In social *salons* wise on Orient Art—
Or laughing in the close congested stalls
At Zimmermann and Bowrey " taking calls."

Or of flower decked Pelitian board the soul
Wit-pitted 'gainst the banter of our Cole,—
When Lobo, or the Dagmar stringed combine,
Arouse the bumper brimming " Auld lang syne."

And by the Bandstand where the horses wait
Close clustered by the Strand's orchestral gate,—
Between the twilights, while the shadows grow
For squealing Gordons swaggering to and fro :—

When William's ramparts loom empurpled black
Against the night-rack piled behind their back,
And river, road, and fort and firmament
In day's gold splash of splendid death are blent.

For four and forty years you 've fought with wrong
And done the State high service all along :—
And won't forget our Ochterlonian skies
When sworded Edward bids "Sir Robert" rise.

Good bye, dear Sir, Calcutta's heart's adieu
Goes to the man who's battled and won through,—
With right good will she speeds your homeward way—
Adieu ! Adieu ! Rampini's off to-day.

The Journal, 30*th August*, 1908.

I KNOW A BANK WHERE BY THE WILD TRAM GOES.

(An old song re-set.)

O ! I am the *War Cry O,*
In the *Kubbu-ka-kargus* van,—
In a couple of Nos. I stood alone
And by No. VII, I ran :
And the Bankers all around
Smiled an irreproachable smile
That heightened the joy of my* editor boy
For I *am* so mercantile !

---

* Mr. Cyril H. Champkin.

For he has a nimble pen
  That can prance for an afternoon
In turning out verse that might well be worse
  Or in etching a crisp cartoon.
And we're all of us quite bedazed
  By his high oratorical style
When he dazzles our wits while our 'Parliament' sits
  For he is so volatile!

O! I am the *War Cry O*,
  And he is the editor rare,
(I've a wrap serene of a sad sap green
  With a weird vignette of the Square.)
And we'll both of us coruscate
  For a very perceptible while
And scintillate smartly for M—l and H—y
  For they *are* so mercantile.
    Yes we *are* so mercantile
      (In an imperturbable style)—
    We'll sin till late nicely and do it precisely
    For *we* are so mercantile.
      Yes *we* are so mercantile.

The Mercantile War Cry,—October 1908.

GAZETTED!

"Captain F. M. L......e becomes Major and Lieut. A. E. Martlli y·(herlh)? loacbaT ountin,O.2."—The "Englishman," 3rd October, 1908.

O hark ye th' latist—
  Th' latist an' greatist,
O hark ye th' latist, now do—
  By th' mountains o' marnin'
He's been that discarnin'
  Sure now he's purradin' O.2.!

His noime sure its Martlli
  He's gettin' on smartly,
He's been decorated—hurroo!
  An' now he's gazetted
An' feted an' petted
  Y-(herlh? loacbaT ountin, O.2.!

Och! the C. V. R.'s boomin'
He'll soon be assoomin'
Th' nixt regimintal digree—
We'll arl be a strummin'
On Martlli's becomin'
Y-(herlh ? loacbaT ountin, O.3.

So wave the shillelah
You've got to roise y-(herlhy
If wishful to match him aloive—
Some folks ignorantly
Assert I'm no Santley—
But I'll sing of O'Martlli O.5.!

The Empire, 8th October 1908.

THE NEW TOWN HALL.

At to-morrow's meeting of the Corporation, Mr. Phelps will move:

(1) That with reference to the surplus land fronting on Hogg Street visible from Chowringhee and the maidan, it is highly desirable that it should be built upon in a manner worthy of the neighbouring buildings now being erected.

(2) That a Committee be appointed to consider what action should be taken with regard to handing over to Government the present Town Hall for a sum that will enable the Corporation to erect another Hall on their own land.

(Whatever may be done or said
The dear Town-hall is never dead.)

Mr. Phelps (*Loquitur.*)

MEN of the moment, men of might,
The hour is come, I'm ready,—
So sink your differences to-night
And take your fences steady!

We've got to fill that surplus bit
Of India wasting sadly,
And, now I come to think of it,
We want a Town-hall badly.

So men of mettle, men of might,—
Just set yourselves to thinking
We'll get the money, fill the site—
And kill two birds like winking!

Our local Whiteley, none too soon,
  A great big shop's erecting—
(I saw the place this afternoon
  When I was round prospecting.)

I strongly urge you, one and all,
  To go at once and view it,
And stimulate our new Town-hall
  To try to live up to it.

There is no doubt about the site,
  (I trust the fact you're gripping)
As a *Bon Marché's* satellite
  The Town-hall will look ripping.

So Jaun Bazar's "*le dernier cri*,"
  Don't let the district fret us,
Let's whole the Hogg and put to sea—
  Oh let us! let us!! let us!!!

The Empire, 13*th October*, 1908.

THE MERRY MILLINER.

(A reprint of Mrs. Eliza Fay's "Original letters from India," with a preface by the Rev. W. K. Firminger is on the point of publication.)

GOOD people all! look out, I pray,
  For "Mrs. Fay" is out to-day—
(Or else to-morrow,) so they say,
In dainty Thackeresque array.
Good people all! now don't be deaf
To Mr. F. and "Mrs. F."
Go buy, go buy, and don't go by,—
You may not get her by and by!
For "Mistress Fay" was quite *au fait*
To all the wits of Warren's day—
She flirted with sleek Macrabie—
And made a bonnet business pay.

(Man's most momentous 'chievements stop
Where's Babel? where that bonnet shop?)
Upon her goods she used to stick a
Card "all in this row nine rupees, sicca."

She even let such titles worry her
As "Ooltapoolta-Ooloobarria,"
"The Alipur," "La Respondentia,"
"La Grand," (but no, she didn't mention her.)
"The Talleyrand," "The Sunda Bunda."
"The Tolly toque—nullah secunda,"
"The Aylmer," and "Le Dernier Ton"—
"As worn by La Belle Sanderson."
("The Eardley Nort—? That's not a hat—
Now who do you think you're getting at?)

She came to India overland—
(Don't mix her up with Mrs. Grand)
But lucklessly became the prey
Of Hyder Ali on the way—
(He never tried to Hyder though
For Ali was quite *comme il faut*—
And no-one ever tried to cut her
At Calicut or Kalicutta.)
It seems that she was Hyder's loot
At Calicut upon the *route*—
Her husband was of no repute
And casually got the boot,
But Mrs. F. was far too cute
To bother much about the brute.

(I hope I don't the tale forget
I haven't read "the letters" yet.

Her letters—she was most sincere—
Misplace the site of Belvedere,
(And several too pedantic prudes
Quote other inexactitudes—
The charge I fear is all too true.)
She said the house was quite *bijou*
Where Hastings lived with "Number Two"—
(A rather curious thing to do.)
(I think that it would be too bad
To hold that Hastings play'd the cad.—
We mustn't at our Warren scoff
For Marian's spouse remarked "I'm hoff!—"
(It was the funny way they had
When Hastings Impey was a lad.)

She saw (Oh bless her pretty eyes !)
Our Busteed's *bustee* on the rise,
And noted every form and phase
Of Busteed's *bustee's* little ways.
What time when all that smouldering fuel
Blazed up that lead to Hastings' duel—
When Francis met a sad mishap—
(The spot is found on Upjohn's map)—
She heard " the Begum " with her hookah
Talk " Charnock's bride "—(they meant to cook her)
And reeled off quite a telling lot
Of journalese upon the spot—
The kind of stuff that could not fail
To get into the *Daily Mail*,
Were *Daily Mails* invented then,
She flourished such a facile pen—
(The sort of folk who write like her
  Cement the " Pax Britannica.")

So " Mistress Fay " don't fail to get
For if you do you may regret—
She's *chaperoned* quite *trés jolie*
By Mister Firminger, B. D.
She's made her *chaperon* her own—
(Ring Thackers up by telephone)
Beneath (in plain or fancy dress)
The *Ægis* of the C. H. S.

I only wish her statues ran
At intervals on the *maidan*.—
Which ever way you try to size her
A girl of parts was fair Eliza.

The Englishman, 27th October, 1908.

TO AN ABSENTEE LEADER.

(A lay of the Lobby.)

MISTER Senator D. was a sensible man,
  Who, when the* Parliament House began
Re-modelled his style on a popular plan—
As a full front-bencher and led in the van.

---

* " The Calcutta Parliament. "

But soon, too soon, so the minute-books say
His feelings cooled off for the Y. M. C. A.—
And once when the House had a "Ladies'" day—
He made it a matter of stopping away.

Did Senator D., as some might suppose,
Make off to the "Saturday Club" *tableaux*—
Forsaking the "Ayes," (there is no-one who knows,
To the "noes" who followed the party nose?

O, Senator D., this gives one pain,
Don't womanœuvre like that again—
Or the figure you danced it is perfectly plain
May land us all in for the "Ladies' chain."

Tableaux, or wherever an absentee goes
On Parliament nights, are but frivolous shows—
And what would become of the Fen Boroughs
If ever your quorumless capering grows.

Think on Horniman's dulcet delectable tones,
And the nightingale numbers of jocular Jones,
Pat Lovett orating with banjo and bones,
And an absentee lobby whom nobody owns.

Dear Senator D., excuse my rubs,—
Do tug yourself off from say Saturday Clubs
On Fridays, or people who thump on the tubs
May let in the women or shut up the pubs.

For Goodwin can wrestle with liquified lakhs,
And Blair may be there with unmatchable "Max,"
And Champkin may spout him perturbable fac's
All nicely assorted and done up in packs.

The season is with us, the speaker in chair,
The *rendez-vous* fixed on in Dalhousie Square,
The call of the lobby is loud on the air
If you cannot turn up, then, for goodness sake, pair.

Mr. Senator D., you can scoop in *éclat*
From the bench to the left of the suave Apcar—
So why should you frivol and frolic afar?—
It isn't the thing for a Parliament Star.

Come lay yourself out in the Parliament line—
You can postulate well, you can perorate fine,—
(One week we were "eight" and we might have been "nine")
Do turn on the gas do, Duchesne, do shine.

HO! IEROE.

(ADAPTED.)

"Although my recovery is much slower than I expected, I am not without hope that I may again take an active part in public life."

Mr. Joseph Chamberlain to the West Birmingham Liberal Unionist Association, 9th October 1908.

With all their banners bravely spread—
And all their armour flashing high—
Saint George might waken from the dead
To see Mid-England's banners fly.

(Adapted.)

HAIL to the cause that to triumph advances!—
Hail to the Chief of the oncoming fray!—
Long may the fire from his eye-glass that glances
Hearten to wisdom the sense of the day.
Heaven send him strength anew.
Earth lend him fighters true—
Mighty to reason, come friend or come foe,
While all of Englishmen
Send up a prayer again
Chamberlain! Chamberlain!

Ho! Ieroe!

Ours is no stripling chance caught in the moulding—
Kinging at Birmingham—London in shade—
Though the whirlwind hath stripped many seats of his holding,
Not yet shall the star of our Chamberlain fade.
Moored to the Midland rock,
Proof to the battle shock—
Firmer he roots him the louder it blow,
North, south, and east and west
Stand to their loved and best
Joseph of Birmingham,—

Ho! Ieroe!

Proudly our banners have flapped their undoing
(Birmingham's cheers to our slogan replied):—
Manchester, Peckham, are smoking in ruin—
And the stalwarts of Asquith are whelmed in the tide.

[o

Clifford and "F. C. G."
Blanch at our contumely—
Winston, the Welshman, and Hardie and Co.—
  Turn the whole rabble out
  Lift the exultant shout
Joseph (and Austen too)

Go Higher Joe.

Poll voters, poll, for the death of the dumper,
  Strain all your powers in prosperity's cause—
Make winning on winning a mandate—a thumper—
  For free handed trading not one sided laws.
Onward to victory—
Ever your earnest cry—
"Wage for the workers, and work!" (thanks to Joe).
  Come again, Chamberlain,
  Lead as of old again,—
England is true to thee,

Ho! Ieroe!

The Journal, 8th November, 1908.

THE THIN END OF THE WEDGE

A newspaper suggestion by "Dak" to build a new Town-hall, on the model of that at Birmingham, on the site occupied by General Outram's Statue in Chowringhee, met with approval in many quarters.

I like to cogitate upon
  The ins and outs about the hall—
To prove the *pro* and con the *con*
  And end the business once for all.
So here you have my little dream
For working out a likely scheme.

Sell Jaun Bazar at hammer's fall
  For flats and *suites*, all neat and nice,—
And hand the coin and tottering hall
  To Government—that's my advice—
And set the Corporation free
Of all responsibility.

The new L.-G. would duly plan
  And build two halls (and there you are)
The one upon the big *maidan*—
  The other North of Bow Bazar.
And when the bills were paid and done
There'd be two halls instead of one.

At just the cost we'd have to face
  For one upon the scented site
That hurtles near to Hogg, his place,
  Which Mr. Phelps thinks quite all right.
And further more I beg to state—
A flat is apt to yield a rate.

The site and hall in Esplanade
  Would sell to build the *maidan* pile,
And Jaun Bazar for sale displayed
  Would all pan out in decent style.
(The Indians in the open meet
And do not want a closed retreat.)

The Outram site is far the best,
  (By Outram you get "Out o'the tram")
The clubs are close, from east and west
  The world, his wife, and children cram
To hob and nob and shoulders rub
Just opposite the U. S. Club.

I strolled on the Marine Parade
  Of Slowcum-Podger-Super-Mare,
At ninety-something in the shade,
  And found it rather *gurrum*, there ;—
Thought I, across the beach I'll skip
And in the briny have a dip.

I met a curious haggard man
  Of haunted and dejected mien,
From whom I hired a bathing-van
  (He called it a "marine-machine.")
I said "cheer up!" "confide in me!"
"Whatever can the matter be?"

"Thim swimming baths," he made reply,—
  "Oop theer oopon tha 'Esplanade,
Will drain tha bloomin' ocean dry
  And swaller oop me bloomin' trade."—
He smote his brow and shook his head;
"Tha thin ind of tha Widge!" he said.

I saw he was of sense bereft
  To cherish such a childish whim,
And said the sea had water left
  Enough for baths as well as him.
" Thim thin idged baths will by and by "
(Said he) " mop arl the ocean dry !"

I strolled along Chowringhee wide
  Beside the oval island site—
Where General Outram takes a ride
  And looks as though his horse would bite.
I said, said I, " whate'er befall,—
Why that's the place for our Town-hall."

I met a busy public man,
  Who said he'd made a scheme his own
To formulate a little plan
  And kill two '*chirrias*' " with one stone "
(I call the people " skinny geese "
Who grudge poor birds a stone a-piece.)

Said he " we've got the land (our own),
  " Shop soiled, a bit upon the shelf,"—
And then he talked about that stone—
  (I'm economical myself.)
" The Hall—the Land in Jaun Bazar !—
You chuck the stone and there you are ! "

I told him of the island site
  With Outram prancing like a Turk—
He said that most distinctly, quite,
  The island project would'nt work.—
I answered " Why ?" He shook his head
" The thin end of the wedge !" he said.

I said " good gracious, my good man !"
  (I talk like that when feeling sore)
" There's miles and miles of good *maidan*—
  " The island gone—there'd miles be more !"
" The thin end of the wedge," he cried,
" Is just the thing we can't abide !"

I said " you want to stick the hall
  Upon a site that wouldn't do—"
" It wouldn't, wouldn't do at all !—"
  He said " Right O, the same to you !"
And then we both began to shout.
(I left him there to think it out).

The Empire, 13th November, 1908.

HOSPITAL SUNDAY.

22nd November, 1908.

THE town was sad and the children cried,
  For the night was long and the heavens afar.
The Angel of Pain spread his pinions wide
  And the pale-steed passed with his sable car.
The healer worked, as the healers do,
  With a hand all love and a heart full sore—
For ever the need of the great town grew
  And ever seemed lesser the healer's store.
The Reaper garnered his meed of gain,
  And the watcher prayed while the worker died—
'Neath the brooding wings of the Angel Pain—
  And that is the reason the children cried.

And the preacher paused in the story old
  (The white robed man with the saintly look)
For he knew that he told what is good to be told
  From the sky-born stores of the glorious Book.
" Give of your plenty—O ye with the hoard !"
  " Give of your poverty ye who are poor !"
" Give—for the pestilence walketh abroad !"
  " Give—for destruction awaits at the door !"
" Give, while 'tis day lest ye ne'er may know"—
  " Give, while ye may or ye ne'er may taste"—
" The joy of 'suaging another's woe"—
  " The strength that comes of a self abased !"

So the teacher ceased and he closed the Book,
  Then turned to the Christ on the painted pane
Where the glad sun swept to the last lit nook
  In a torrent of gold o'er that radiant fane.

And the healers battled with death and disease
   With a cheerier, heartier, vigour I wot
Because of the helpers who learned on their knees
   What the good man told of a self forgot.

The Englishman, 23*rd November*, 1908.

THE DREAM OF KURZON KHAN.

(Another report is shortly expected concerning the Victoria Memorial Hall.)

IN Kalkuttah did Kurzon Khan
   A stately wonder-dome decree:
Where half the sacred *maidan* ran—
In columns measureless to man.
      In nineteen nothing three.
Where twice two miles of verdant ground
With walks and drives were girdled round:
And there were golf-greens bright with tinuous frills
   Where blossomed many a Haskell bearing tee;
And here a race-course redolent of ills
   Regarding sunny lawns of raillery.*

But oh, that long romantic grove† which slanted
   Down the green turf toward the hidden river!
A pleasant place, as lonely and enchanted
As e'er beneath cathedral bell was haunted
   By maiden waiting for her prayer-book'd lover!
And from this grove, with ceaseless turmoil seething,
As if the earth in stick-fast-bricks were breathing,
   A mighty platform momently was forced:
   Amid whose swift (now interrupted) burst
Huge fissures faulted to resounding hail
Of grinning chaff beneath the mocker's flail;
   And past these prancing bricks at once and ever
   Was flung by momently the sacred river,
For miles meandering with a mazy motion
   By *hát* and *ghát* the sacred river ran,
   Then reached the Sund-Bunds measureless to man,
And sank in tumult to a mudless ocean:
   And 'cross this tumult Kurzon heard from far
   "Max"-estral voices 'jaculating *Wah!*

---

* A newspaper discussion was going on about the dividing of the lawn in front of the grand-stand by a railing, thus creating two classes of public spectators.

† The selected site of the Hall is that of the avenue leading from the Cathedral towards the Hughli.

The promise of the dome at leisure
  Floated somewhere in the skies;
While was heard the mingled measure
  Of the "wherefores?" and the "whys?"
It was a miracle of sound advice
A marble-wonder-dome with paves of price.

A damsel with a dulcimer
(India symbolised) I saw:
  It was an Anglo-Indian maid
  And of our dull delays she played,
Singing of Queen Victoria.
  Could I recall unto you
Her sympathy and song,
  To such a deep disgust 't would woo you
That to plaudits loud and long,
  We would build that dome so fair,
That marble dome those paves of price.
  And all the world should see them here,
  And none would cry "Beware beware!
  Her flashing eyes, her floating hair!"
Weave Reports around it thrice?—
  Oh, stay your pen and know instead
  That we upon Reports are fed
And want the Hall. We've got the pice.

The Journal, *29th November*, 1908.

TO G. E.

(A rejoinder to "TO MEN" by "G. E." in the *Empire* of the previous day.)

WELL put, fair lady, neatly writ—
  Mere man collapses like a jelly
Before a style that breathes the wit
  That stamps the caste of M. Corelli—
You've told us all creation's *gup*
With Bobbie Burns to back you up.

We know we're Nature's "coarser clay"
  Spell-bound before a plaster Venus—
All faulty, rough, and strange (you say)
  With scarce a shred of sense between us.
Of course we're Nature's sole misfit—
But is it well to harp on it?

You say He "made fair woman last"—
He did, he did (the saints forfend us),
She's lasted through the ages past—
Her staying powers are just tremendous—
"Shaped from a purer fairer clay."
(Mud man, of course, must needs obey.)

When Nature tried her prentice best
And fangled forth our callow race—
While Adam proved a week-end jest—
Eve popped up with a smiling face—
And vexed his soul with chaff *ad lib*
Concerning an elusive rib.

That rib's the rub that Bob forgot
When singing of "the lassies, o"—
If Adam was a sorry lot
'Twas scarce for Eve to tell him so.
Man's merits wear a trifle thin,
Then why, fair lady, rub them in?

It seems to some but shallow good
To wide the gulf that parts the sexes—
To buz about in waspy mood
And vex the chap who pays the exes.
Though warped the way and wild the weather
The Eden pair should pull together.

'Tis well to con the storied page
On snake and fruit in old Genasis—
To plumb its lessons and to gauge
Their trend on philosophic basis,—
Th' evicted *malli* and his wife
Went out—but 'hand-in-hand'—for life.

Go weave a "garland of love lays"
Or tune your lyre to "songs of passion"—
And lead us by Gladysian ways
In well approved expressive fashion,—
Our faults are due to "structural" tricks
So why come down on us like bricks?

The Empire, 16*th December*, 1908.

TO WINSTON IN THE OLD LION'S DEN.

(See also O. S. in *Punch*, 20th January, 1909.)

"I do not suppose that a great city has ever fallen into the grasp of such a narrow-minded set of politicians. In their political opinions we can discover no single generous principle of government or philosophy, nothing but push, grab and caucus from start to finish. They have deserted one party to pervert the other."

(Mr. Winston Churchill at Birmingham.)

AND this from you in that same Midland hall
  Where he was wont to voice his city's aim,
Her wise to rally,—trumpet-tongued, to call
  Her sons to duty in fair wisdom's name.

From you, who reap the red apostate's meed,
  A turncoat babbler when all's said and done,
You, officed blusterer of grabbing greed,
  You, advertiser arch of Number One.

"No single principle of generous aim
  Has marked his course encaucussed from the start"—
From you pert pervert of chameleon fame,
  Of tongue to cheek and outspread hand to heart.

As child, I saw him on the hustings stand
  In '68, a stripling fighter fit,
By Bright lion-headed, and an eager band,
  His townsmen,—scan the record they have writ.

A fungus town, far stretched a vestried sore,—
  To England's shame,—to vice and ills a prey,
The young lion furious raised resistless roar
  And set his teeth to gnaw the wrong away.

Then lesser lions soon ranged them to his trail
  To hound a jackal pack to outer night—
And fur flew freely where the young lion's tail
  Lashed long and lordly in resounding fight.

And so it came that evil fell away,
  Right ruled, and bumbled dotage toppled slain—
Mid-England's city crowns the land to-day—
And where's the cur to snarl at Chamberlain?

I saw him, Mayor, first don the City's chain,
  I saw him voted to the School-board chair,
And twice the Mayoral call he heard again
  E'er yet I saw him borne to Westminster.

And then from Palace-yard his roar was caught
  In deeper, fuller tones of mellowed age,—
And twice his vantage reckoned but as nought
  He stepped from power to whiten History's page.

And, you, the sucking-dove who roars amain,—
  So that men laugh to hear a pigeon shout,
And tell each other "let him roar again!"
  Nor care, like you, what 'tis you roar about—

Succeed, say some, to starred viceregal robe—
  And look, enthroned, to weave the Orient's fate,
The keyless wards of inmost East to probe
  And swing the portals of her hingeless gate.

T'unmesh the web that taxed a Canning's skill,
  That random Ripon failed him to unlace,
That all but broke steel-handed Dufferin's will.
And harassed Curzon from his pride-of-place.

This you essay, with shrill impetuous cry
  (Fine prelude to hot youth's adventurous pose)
Anent the strengthless lion with glazing eye
  All battle-broken at a gallant close.

Well, well, you're young, and words are but as wind,
  They fill a Reuter'd column gaping wide.
When once you've left the Asquith crowd behind
  And passed the cut that leads to Suez side—

You'll yet have days and days to con the tale
  Of India's past, so read and reading wonder,
And then may-hap 't won't be without avail
  For India, greeting on th' Apollo Bunder.

If, when, put off viceregal harness high,
  You go where Rulers go, who go and come,
You've done for great Calcutta, by and by,
  A tithe the good "Joe" did for "Birminggum"—

We won't enlarge upon your "narrow mind,"
  Your "push and grab," nor fling your failings at you,—
To your full lack of generous instincts blind
  In Winston Park we'll raise a Churchill statue.

21*st February*, 1909.

THANKS,—BANKS!

"At present Mr. D'Cruz's motto seems to be 'cui bono?' I would recommend as a change 'nil desperandum.'"

We take the above neat little philosophic tabloid from Dr. Banks' latest minute on the New Market. It is, however, susceptible of a wider application!

The Empire, *4th March*, 1909.

THOSE views
On Cruz
Make pleasant news
Now times are out of joint—
He's made a hit
With grace and grit
And touched d'cruzial point.
He recommends
To all his friends
A change of Civic motto
"CUI BONO?"
NO!
That's quite *de trop*
We'll out another trot—o.
Whate'er time bring
It's now the thing
At last, at length (*ad tandem*)—
In a good cause to sing aloud
In a good cause and a big crowd
To shout
"NIL DESPERANDUM

The sun, the moon and asteroids
Think well of Dr. B.'s tabloids—
With peckers up they play the game
And go on going—just the same—
The while he bangs the big boss drum
To advertise his fine nostrum.
So don't despair,—
Keep on your hair,—
In life's bright lexicon for sale
There's never no such word as
FALE.

With wonder wrought
The mighty thought
Springs from his cerebellum.—
It ought to be chalked up all round

Wherever billstickers abound—
It ought to out-flame at night
From lofty Ochterlony's height—
(Or else engrossed on vellum.)
But let come what
Come may, his mot—
—to's not
Half bad, so go it—
Buck up, buck up, forbear to frown,
Let care cark on, bid worry drown,
We'll ne'er be down
About our town
Or, if we are, won't show it,—
(Not if we know it).

The Empire, 4th March, 1909.

LOOKING NORTH.

(The previous issue of the *Empress* contained two views of the Cathedral and Government House from the Ochterlony Monument "looking north.")

O! *Empress* of my hearth and home—
("My hearth" in Ind's a mere convention)
I've bound you as a serial tome
Year in, year out, I'm proud to mention;
Whate'er betide you gaily thrive,
Your last (June 2) came welcomed gladly,—
Until on lighting on page 5
I found myself unsettled badly.

I snatched a *topé* from the rack
And started off on Shanks his pony—
(A quite convenient sort of hack)
To climb the lofty Ochterlony:
Though stairs are things I can't abide
When bats abound begrimmed and burly—
(It's rather dark when you're inside
And everything goes twirly whirly).

The top at last as morning broke
To Phœbus' call (he's always game for it)
I took a dial from my poke—
(A compass is the better name for it).

Though perched above familiar ground
The north (you name) seemed more than misty
While panoramas all around
Just like the stairs went twisty wisty.

There southward gleams a gothic spire
(Your *north* just gives of Paul's a hinto)
And, here, those walls we all admire
That cost a mint and shelter Minto.
And there the spot Macaulay knew
Where club the cream of all the best to-day,—
With *façade* bulged a quaint askew
Not as 'of yester—but of eschterday.

By *Empire* Bandmann's dome arise
The Hotel Grand's aspiring glories
That eat the earth and cloak the skies
At something less than fifteen stories.
While a *Bon Marche's* scaffold show
Gives hope of flat at decent *rentum*
And smacks of bargains row on row
Each redolent of eight *per centum.*

Lo, the Hogg market's clockless height
Our new rialto's campanille,
('Twill later be illumed at night
Whate'er the weather grill or chill-y.)
And t'other tower where *ediles* sit
When Wednesdays yield a floor of fussing
(*The Empress* off descants on it—
See 'tolycus Autolycussing.)

Where statues dot the village green
(That boasts a vista casuarina)
Is Bobs-in-bronze erect serene
(Though "Max" asserts he might be cleaner).
And far on the horizon's brink
Rise mystic corrugated oddities—
And men there be who sometimes think
It was a hall, but don't know what it is.

All these I saw from where I stood—
Yet gazing to the *north* you tell of,
Could nowhere trace the prospects good
You evidently think so well of.

"The east is east and west is west"
Writes Kipling casually cynical,
That south's not north is now confessed,—
I've proved it from the *maidan's* pinnacle.

The Empress, July, 1909.

THE PILL, THE PILL, AND NOTHING BUT THE PILL.

(Mr. Beecham, the celebrated pill-maker, has contributed £300,000 to the National Opera House Fund.)

TO save "the Duchess" * from the Yanks
A hat went on the rounds,
Till some-one earned the nation's thanks
With forty thousand pounds.

This forty thousand pounder will
Feel small now its about
That Beecham of the wondrous pill
Has come and cut him out.

The cork-screw's mightier than the sword,—
The pill outvies the two,
For lakhs from laxatives afford
A new found point of view.

The man unmoved by music's spell
—By concord of sweet sounds—
Forgot his stratagems to tell
Three hundred thousand pounds.

Sweet are the uses of advert—
—isment, so all may hope,—
Though bitter-sweet the tastes that flirt
With aloes and with soap.

When *Il Dinora's* "Shadow Dance"
The proud proscenium thrills,
La Diva owes her happy chance
To some-one-else's pills.

---

* Holbein's portrait of the Duchess of Milan in Trafalgar Square.

For rhubarb rules the boards at last
  (It's now a settled fac')
And wags the stick for Wagner's cast,
  Or Merry Offenbach.

Taraxacum up-lifts the roof,
  Its voice a riftless lute—
Podophyllin requires no proof
  With note beyond dispute.

The singer struts the tuneful stage
  Or lolls between the wings—
A marionette in puppet age
  When pilules pull the strings.

Fling wide the light, in dance gyrate
  Nor let the *bâton* drop—
Bid all the world appreciate
  The nation's chemist's shop ;—

The Pill of Fancy and of Fate
  Moves operatic man—
Till regal Death manipulate
  His curtained rat-a-plan.

Three hundred thousand pounds planked down
  For buskins and for socks !—
(A stall should cost us half-a-crown,—
  A box—*a guinea-a-box*).

The Journal, 25th July, 1909.

ONE CHANCE LEFT.

REUTER wires from Copenhagen
  Of the turn that things have taken,
  How that Dr. Cook has travelled
To the hyperborean Pole,—
  And we feel a trifle gravelled
  Now the mystery's unravelled
That so long has vexed the cockles of our speculative soul.

For a person'ly conducted
Cook has blown a Yankee trumpet
  On a spot John Bull intended
Should be gramaphoned by him;—
  Out across the floes he wended
  Till the quest was neatly ended
And he'd spoofed us fair and squarely of a cherished little
    whim.

He drove jolly dogs in legions
To the unenticing regions
  That surround the icy packses
Where the polar bears reside,—
  And disturbed the polar axis
  To elucidate the paraxis
Of an agitated compass when you reach the other side.

By the northern blast unhampered
Round the panorama scampered
  Game to rouse the admiration
Of a smiling Rooseveldt:—
  And we make our salutation
  To the star-bespangled nation
For we're sure he'd not have done it had he thought of what
    we've felt.

Beneath the red Aurora
That illumes the Arctic *flora*
  Bears, dogs, and seals were gracious.—
Though it must have been a shock
  To the *fauna* unvoracious
  That patrol the landscape spacious
When that party came prospecting from the wilds of An-
  natok.

Cook returned to Upernivik
And evoked a welcome civic
  From the local Corporation
With the fire-brigade and mace;
  And Bull met the information
  With the terse ejaculation
That he reckoned Upernivik was a silly sort of place.

A Frenchman flew the Channel
With his head tied up in flannel
  And transformed our island holding
Into a peninsula—
  And one tends a bit to scolding
  At the prospect that's unfolding
Of the interloping foreigner a-taking things too far.

The Frenchman flew to Dover,
And the Polar boom is over,
  And William slapped Zeppelin
On the back in gay Berlin—
  While the Sunday-schools were yellin'
  And the petrol-tanks a-smellin'
To the "Hochs!" asseverated 'mid the Deutscher-throated
    din.

Now there's little we can tackle
For Lieutenant Mr. Shackle-
  ton has got to turn attention
To a "Dreadnought" for a-while.
  It's a horrid thing to mention
  But it seems the fixed intention
Of the Yank and Frank to bluff us and to cut us out in
    style.

May gallant Cody winging
On to Manchester be bringing
  Luck to British aviation
Damped by plucky Blériot.—
  And a later wired narration
  May deny the confirmation
Of the story of the dog-teams and the brace of Eskimo.*

Yet Bull may cease repining
That his chances are declining
  To bewitch the world to wonder
And restore his sinking star,—
  Let him ruminate and ponder
  On the glory waiting yonder
For the man who probes the reaches of the newer New
  Bazar.

---

* It did.

Make your will out most minutely,
Name your exors. most astutely,
  Ere you brave the vista yawning
Dear to Bertram, Banks, and paint,—
  Fame hunting heed no warning—
  But just go there some fine morning
And you may emerge a hero—only then perhaps you mayn't.

The Journal, 5th September 1909.

THE APOTHEOSIS OF THE ANT.

IT was a wily White Ant that I saw a-passing by—
  A personable White Ant with a twinkle in his eye,—
I knew him in a moment for I'd heard of him before—
A comprehending creature with discriminating maw.

His the air of calm absorption of the folk who ever win,
He never sticks at obstacles but always takes them in,
And he dwells in sleek seclusion with the *duftries* and the cats
In the mild and mildewed precincts of the Secretariats.

Precursor of Postponement, the Apostle of Delay,
(You should always do to-morrow what you ought to do to-day),
He deals in devastation and dabbles near and far
In the eating up of records till we don't know where we are.

We patter and we potter and we postulate and pose
With a fundamental leaning to a shelving at the close,
Then we shunt the serried schedules with a qualified demur
To the *duftries* and the kittens who expostulate and purr.

You may see in him the symbol of the "why ?" of Ind's decay—
The emblem of progression in a retrogressive way—
Our motto "words not action" we but seldom "touch the spot,"
Then we file our "resolutions" and he gobbles up the lot.

The Tiger stood for India in far off days that were—
A necked heraldic Tiger with a dominating air;
Though long there's been a better beast to represent our style—
That plodding pushfnl potentate—the penetrating Byle.

Forget the tawny Tiger and the Byle with crumpled horn,
And pass the mad Mosquito by with supercilious scorn—
To hail the wily White Ant with his desiccating charms
As the right heraldic fellow to surmount our coat-of-arms.

In London's central city where the omnibuses range
A cricket tops the summit of the lofty Royal Exchange ;—
Let us decorate the apex of our Ochterlony high
With a wily Ant *prancété proper* up against the sky—
  A warrantable White Ant with a twinkle in his eye.

For why ? Our wants are many, we may get them by a fluke
When Winston's an Archbishop with Lloyd George a Duke.

The Journal, 12*th September* 1909.

CHERANGI AD LEONES.

(During the last few days the central dome of the New Bengal Club has been flanked by a pair of Lions.)

OH, we are the couple to lighten
  The gloom of the town in the rains,
To cheer up Chowringhee and brighten
  The world with our might and our manes,—
Unassailable lions of Calcutta—
The latest and greatest on view,
  A remarkable brace
  Of unqualified grace
Of the local and leonine zoo.

To lounge on a ledge at your leisure
  By a wonderful dome in the sky,
And laugh at the place is a pleasure
  To folk who are built to live high.—
As stuck-up and stucco'd observers
Who posture and pose as they ought—
  Why each of us thinks
  He's a classical sphinx
And tries to live up to the thought.

Oh shade of the author of "Vanit"—
  "—y Fair" how the motors fly by,
With the street at our paws we can scan it—
  Twin critical cynics on high.—
Oh, shades of Macaulay and Thackeray,
We're the pride and the talk of the town—
  An ineffable pair
  With our nose in the air,
And we never intend to come down.

The inferior lions of the city,
  Poor fellows, are left in the lurch,
Our *salaams* with a fathomless pity,
  From a quite unapproachable perch.
Apt Apcar is rigid with envy,
And Allen is off to Bombay,
  And Bertram and Banks
  And the scrawlers and cranks
Are thinking of creeping away.

There is no-one, no no-one can teach us—
  They may post us effusions in packs,
No preacher nor prophet can reach us,
  Not even unmatchable "Max."
Who tilts at us tilts to confusion,
E'en Galstaun would ride for a fall,
  Though stiff in the joints
  We can give them all points
For we are the lions on the wall.

On Kellner's one gloats with precision,
  To Paul's is the other's outlook,
And the flippant in waggish derision
  Have christened us "Peary" and "Cook."
For we are the lions of Calcutta,
Of the hour and the town as a whole,
  At the hub of the club
  We can pull off each rub—
The lions at the top of the poll.

The Journal, 3rd October 1909.

CAVE CANEM.

(*A Dog and Bull story.*)

Noble Spaniel (answering to the name of "Marquis.") "They tell me that as a sportsman I ought to tackle this thing (the "People's Budget"), but I'm not at all sure I shan't let it pass." (Vide *Punch*, Cartoon, 6th October, 1909.)

(*Spaniel Loquitur.*)

A dog's chance, Punchius, you have put it short
In your inimitable way cartoony,—
This little dog's not laughing at such sport
This afternoony.

I am "Sir Oracle," and when I ope
My lips to bark why then let no bull bellow;
(He 'll take the hint and go away I hope
The hulking fellow.)

I hold the realm within my hollow'd paw—
The Chamberlains and Chaplin love to coax me,
And Rosebery rubs me up and down with awe
And Balfour strokes me.

End me or mend me! What a beast to turn!
Massed maunds of muscle, how shall I get round him?
Horn, hoof and hide with mischief all aburn—
The brute, confound him!

I'll—I'll be muzzled if I ever struck
A tighter corner since I took to mauling,
Each dog's a day to call his own, worse luck,
This day's appalling.

Look at his head, and hear his horrid snort,
And watch his tail a-lashing and a-larking,
By Sirius, it's serious this sort,
Its no use barking.

My bark's worse than my bite he seems to say,
—And doesn't care a straw that I am furious,
The other bulls I worried ran away,—
This one's so curious.

Though but a spaniel I have done my share
Of biting and of fighting for my feeding—
I sent a "Temperance" steer for change of air—
A dog of breeding.

And when the "Education" oxen came
My coronet! I gave their tails a twisting,
We've heard the last of what d'you call the game—
Passive Resisting?

But here's a whopper, strolled from Asquith's farm,
A braggart, bullying, blundering, bungling "Budget,"
No dog's a chance in atmosphere so warm—
I think I'll trudge it—

With tail between my legs and nose in air,—
Let Art and Commerce, Laws and Learning die,—
This beastly "Budget" isn't my affair
(He's following by the by.)

What *shall* I do? He's coming on behind,
Slap through the hedge and leave the blatant Bos up?
Or should I turn and face the beggar blind?
Its just a toss up!

24th October 1909.

LONDON THE KEY.

"I remember Lord Beaconsfield's memorable truth that the 'Key to India is London' and that the control of the destinies of India rests largely with the qualities of the British race."—LORD ROSEBERY at Edinburgh, 19th October 1909.

THE truth, my Lord, the truth and nought beside,
The deed-rock of our rule that can't be undone,
The Lord of Hughendon's much mouthed aside—
"The key to India—London."

You take us back to days when England led
The world and said she always meant to do it;
Strong Egypt rose, a Lazarus from the dead,—
Constantinople knew it.

When war-flushed Russia trained her guns to break
Or bend the Turk to Muscovite aggression,
'Twas Beaconsfield who kept our wits awake
Within and out of session.

Broke Gladstone at the "bag and baggage," game,
  Curbed Bright with "perish India," glib precursor
Of Chamberlain of "toil-less lily" fame—
  Each a Lloyd-George, or worser.

When pulpits shook to platform'd rabble rot
  Like "force no remedy," and mob ran riot,
He put it "shall we rule, or shall we not?"—
  Its "England Up" be quiet!"

Apt to outphrase the rhetorician's flight—
  The sophist with verbosity o'erladen—
He singly won for England in a night
  The road that flows to Aden.

Our thanks, my Lord, for this the latest pearl
  Ploughed from the lonely furrow where you wander,
A lustre'd relic of the wizened Earl,—
  Word-gem on which to ponder.

In this mad whirl of mingled froth and guile,
  Of "mended-council-acts" to make one shudder,
You've re-unlocked the key we'd lost awhile—
  Revealed where swings our rudder.

London the pivot of the Empire still,
  Calcutta suburb, as Quebec or Dulwich,
That's the idea to make and fill the bill—
  The overflow and ullage.

World-spread from Westminster, an Empire firm
  For right and might, there's no escaping from it,
Its on the way, though lesser folk may squirm,
  Like Halley's sky-spread comet.

Let India feel the facts the fool would hide,
  Quench quail, stem storm, and foil the prattling paniccer,
Strong armed within stout borders, flinging wide,
  The Pax Britannica.

One with the West she, voyaging, heads for Light,
  Bulwarked to seas that crush, to skies that scatter.
Self tillered drifts to red chaotic night.—
  —Tho moral of the matter.—

This text is ta'en from thoughtful Rosebery's speech,
  "The Key to India—London"—think, apply it—
The application isn't far to reach
  Its wisdom—who'd deny it?

We've half a million sterling, less or more,
To build a "marble dream" to Ind's laudation
Listless Calcutta thinks the thing a bore
With cracked foundation.

Materialize the "dream" on London's Mall,
Returf the Maidan, let the golfers go it;—
The Key to India's London once for all.—
Does London know it?

The heart of England and of India throbs
Fullest within the radius known to taxis,
Where most fares spend their eightpences and bobs
With Charing Cross as axis.

Lift high the "dream" where London's millions throng
As symbol of the story never olden,
To tell of rightness lording over wrong,
Of dross turned golden.

Pile high the Hall where London's lilacs blow,
And oil the wards to make the Key turn pretty;
Where Curzon's on the spot to run the show
With Emerson's Committee.

The Journal, 24th October 1909.

"MOMENTOUS."

"A 'Gazette of India' Extraordinary, yesterday, notified that the Governor-General in Council, with the approval of the Secretary of State, proclaimed that day as the day on which the Indian Councils Act was to come into operation. The Government concludes its Resolution with these words: 'The Governor-General in Council feels that these momentous changes constitute a generous fulfilment of the gracious intention foreshadowed by the King-Emperor's Message. We have repeatedly insisted, as the Reform Scheme developed, that the Government was giving away priceless prestige in response to clamour from a very small section of the peoples of India. Representative institutions are foreign to the genius of the Oriental, and where they have been tried they have failed."—*The Englishman*, 16th November.

MOMENTOUS! Aye! What change is this to-day?
Why deaf the wise? Why dumb who may not see
The shield of England dulled to sober grey,—
The eyes of England blind, and turned away
From signs portentous of the days to be?

To party passion blind, by brooding fanned
  To folly, at cool reason's empty throne;
To poisoned ignorance and listless land,
To quick sedition stark of venomed gland,
  Garnering her winnowed harvest tempest sown.

The flood-gates open to the thronging tide
  Of tireless ones who talk so talk may flow;
The babbler sits where England kept with pride
The courts of England's honour white and wide,—
  Her scutcheon scatheless fronting friend and foe.

Gone the great age, and lost the golden few
  Who knew to rule as Kings in power and place:
The little folk of faction's bitterest brew
Loom large and larger on the nearing view—
  And ape our England's freedom to her face.

Sect calls to race, and caste and creed combine.
  The tribes go up to name the Councils high.
May figs from thistles spring in fair entwine—
Or silken wallets ear from Circe's kine—
  Or daws of need prevail where eagles fly?

Spin, spin the wheel and let the hustings rage,
  Cram *hat* and *ghat* to full with lust of cries,
The talkers mummers—all the land a stage
Where mimic mouthing mountebanks engage
  In engineering fate in alien guise.

Then bid the west to praise the thing new born,—
  The frankenstein in motley, gendered shrill
Of shreds and patches, rags and tatters torn,
Voiced as the clarion-fowl to wake the morn
  And dominate the wondering millions' will.

Comes wind along the chambers of delay
  In rumbling menace, blown of tongue and pen,
To a dazed empire's glib ranged dis-array
Of tinkling cymbals tinkered to display
  Of brazen corridors of meagre men.

Come claimant weakling and nepotic gift,—
  The placer taking toll of him enstooled;
The closet stairway of the panderer's shift,
Manipulated honour prone to lift
  The grabber, hand to back, above the fooled.

Then pandemonium—rump of vandal hordes.—
  A gagged, out-voted England fain to yield
Her rule to them, the peoples' lawful lords
Who forged her fetters, drawing tight the cords
  To fling her staggering from th' unequal field.

Sect strives with race, with creed and caste at brawl—
  Why deaf the wise ? Why blind the strong to see
The lifting *purdha* as the shadows fall,—
The mortar ravished from the gracious wall,—
  While England sends "Reform" to crush the free ?

And last worn India watching by the wave,
  With hand to brow, her agony confessed,
Crouching to peer where leaping waters lave
The vengeance-bringing squadrons, strong to save,—
  Where ride reclaiming cohorts from the West.

The landing hosts' street welcomed eager stream,—
  Artilleried legions quick to quell the storm,—
Foiled fads, shamed subtilities a mocking dream—
Sharp shivered when the spitting maxims gleam
  To cleave red mouthed the path of true Reform.

The Journal, 21*st November* 1909.

WANDERING QUATRAINS.

NOW looms the counter with its Christmas tale,
  Gaily arrestive on unloitering sale,
Where Oxenham and Percy White compete,
And Golliwogs and Teddy-bears prevail.

Now lures the extra number as of yore,
We *sign curro* and leave with half a score—
  The *Graphic* and the *Strand* and Mr. *Punch*,
With *Omar* and with almanacks galore.

Now comes the "Cleveland" with a final flow
Of western visitors who come and go
  Like shades along the Grand's Car'vanserai
And tie np all our *ticcas* in a row.

Myself Chowringhee's side-walk did frequent
And heard anon accented argument—
On the location of some missed Black Hole,
And what they guessed that *gharry-wallah* meant.

Now glows at eve bright Clubland on the view,
The "U. S." and the "Bengal," and the "New"
As lamps to light our "fittons'" homeward way,—
Though which is which the Yanks don't know,—do you ?

Now pile the tees and whack the brassy cleeks,
Now pass the Gordons, kilted or with breeks,
While papers tell that Smith goes home next May
Each week for weeks and weeks and weeks and weeks.

Listen again. Come Tuesday at the feast
Of Andrew brither Scots throughout the East
Will toast 'tis said "the land in which we lie"—
(For thus the *Statesman* anyhow at least.)

The "missing Mercury" for so I hear,
We lost awhile and looked for far and near
That used to hop alert by Outram's side
Has now turned up, at green groved Belvedere.

Cool nips the morn awisp with filmy fogs,
The Levée beckons, brush your evening togs,
The season's sliding gaberdined in gas
From glib St. Andrew to the barking Dogs.

And when mid sheaves of bills it disappears
A whirling memory of joys and fears,
We'll catalogue it thus—"It knew no Rink—
The gods were kind"—and bid it join the years.

So make the most of all we now discern,
And note the Council's ultimate concern—
The how, the when, the where, the why because,
To cast the die for Apcar or Tremearne.

The "Caledonia's" left, the "Cleveland" waits
To weigh her anchor at our watery gates,
The Lords and Commons topple,—bump—bump—bump,—
Such fun delights the furies and the fate.

The Journal, 23*th November* 1909.

CUPID.*

I cannot tell what this Love may be—
  A beautiful boy with a quiver of darts,
A queer little man in a floricsome glee
  Flinging arrows around to unsettle our hearts.
A blind little fellow of infinite jest
Who beckons and blushes and sits on our chest,
As fickle deceiver without any clothes
All nodding and naked in classical pose.

At his best but a dream of the vivider kind,—
At his worst a lost wail from the back of the wind,—
Though "borne of a Goddesse" he lacketh a lodge
So rambles all over the place on the dodge.
The keys of our senses he takes in disdain,
While his nectar resembles two shilling champagne;
And his red petalled roses all tumble to bits
On a judge and a jury let loose with our '*chits*.'

Yet the lords of the lyre and the lute in his praise
String sonnets and rondeaux and lyrics and lays.
From Chaucer to Herrick, from Raleigh to Keats
To carol his gambols or sigh his defeats.
Though good Lady Hylton has pencilled his pricks,
And, for Newbolt, I've new bolted lots of his tricks—
Yet somehow or other with sorrow I see
I cannot tell what this Love may be.

The Englishman, 13*th December* 1909.

---

* From a review of Lady Hylton's "Book of Cupid," with an introduction by Mr. H. Newbolt.

ROSSCUED.*

THE TALE OF A CADDYASTROPHY.

"A local golfer a few days ago sent his ball into the tank at Tollygunge and his caddy on going into the water to recover it was seized with cramp and called aloud for help. The golfer rescued him in a half drowned condition."—*The Empire.*

HE smote and foozled sadly, so the ball,
An agile Haskell, disappeared a sunker,
For, for the nonce, the tank was what you'd call
A Bunker.

"Lost Ball!" the caddy cried (a valiant lad)
His "sticks" discarded and his *puggree* peeled,
Slap in the tank went flop and got cramp bad
And squealed.

True to the instincts of his kin and clan
He took a header, not to say a plunger,
And rose to the occasion like a man
And Tollygunger.

Across the wave he saw the nipper's nob,
And heard the nipper nipped with cold a-sobbin'
And thought at once he'd obviate a job
For Dobbin.†

He breasted well the wild and watery tank
And nabbed the little nipper by the flipper,
And spread him out to dry upon the bank—
Poor nipper!

Then grabbed a putter and called "Fore,—I'm on!"
His nerve a something simply fine and awesome;—
He holed his Haskell at a stroke and won
A foursome.

---

* "Truth will out, and even at the risk of a raid on the lowlands of Mission Row we find ourselves compelled to divulge the name of the hero of the tank incident at Tollygunge. Apparently 'Dâk's' verses published the other day have led some people to suppose that it was Mr. Norman McLeod who fished his caddy out of the stilly—we should say chilly—waters of the tank at No. 4. As a matter of fact it was his namesake and relative, Mr. Norman Ross. Mr. Ross paid for his dip with a sharp go of fever, but we are glad to hear that he is all right again."—*The Empire* (later).

† The Coroner.

Such men at call of duty never wince,
  To find his like you'd have to make a long quest,—
I don't suppose you'd find one 'fore or since
  The Nor-r-man Conquest!

The Empire, 16th December 1909.

ANN VERONICA.*

A rose was Ann Veronica,
  An Iris or Japonica,
A daisy or a butter-cup or lily of the dells,
  A cocky, hockey girlie—
  (For you have to get up early,
Or sit up late, to estimate the belles of Mister Wells).

  A straight but rather dodgy gal,
  A lady biological
She used to cram, nor muffed exam, but always got a pass.
  Her daddy was belated,
  And her auntie auntiquated,
But none-the-less, I must confess, she loved a looking-glass.

  Yet fate was rough on "A. V."
  When her daddy bellowed "cave!"
The night she tried a "Corsair's Bride" to grace a fancy ball.
  Her notions being jolted
  She slipped away and bolted
To London town, with half a crown,—"Dad wouldn't do at all."

  Alas! for Ann Veronica!
  Lone London proved a tonic-a—
For Ramage, bent on damage, crossed her "A. V."—ating stage,
  But in "Restaurant Rococo"
  Annie banged him on the "boko"—
And "*jiu-jitsu*" hits you when the lady's in a rage.

---

* From a review of "Ann Veronica" by Mr. H. G. Wells.

Then in woe and worry swimmin'
She took up with "Votes for Women!"
With Fabians and Shavians discursive on her track—
Till, her whim evaporated,
She just wired to Dad and waited—
"Ave 'A. V.'—we'll kill the calf"—come answer.
("Vee" went back.)

*   *   *   *   *   *   *

Alas for Ann Véronique—
Her cussedness waxed chronic—
(Love's crimson petals turn to nettles lacking wedding bells)—
With the worst of best intentions
She discarded the conventions—
(This sort of stuff's not good enough,—no thank you Mister Wells).

The Englishman, 20*th December* 1909.

THE SEA QUEEN.*

THERE'S a wealth of waving woodlands where the water-maidens flirt
Loose tresses and anenomies sway softly to and fro—
Oh it's fine to catch the glamour of our Sea-queen's clinging skirt.
A sparkle in the moon-light of her galleries below.

The white sea-horses fume and fret to touch the sea-moon's disc
All afloat in amber lustre in a lilac sea ravine—
And the water-goblins frivol and the hippocampi frisk,
Where the nautilus goes sailing in his ivory barque between.

Brave Ford and Mr. Longmans (not to mention Green and Co.)
May you carry on for ever your chromatic clear design
To enrich the sliding glories of the ages as they glow
With the spell of Andrew's delvings in the lore of auld—"Lang"—syne.

The Englishman, 20*th December* 1909.

---

* From a review of the "Olive Fairy Book" by Mr. Andrew Lang.

THE BOOK-LOVER IN INDIA.

A Sunday, and the '*dâk*' at last
  Stamped with Edvardus Septimus,
The bladed fan is whirring fast,
  (Ah, *asti*, *bearer*—soda—*bus!*)—.
A Sunday, and the mail is in
With home-land missives thick and thin.

A '*chit*' from J. n. s.,—well J. n. s. may wait,
  A price-list from S. G. and Co.,—
A crested screed from B...f. rt. Gate.
  A portrait-card of Clemenceau,—
From Paris stamped with "La Semeuse."
(I'm fond of picture post-card views).

What's this? A portly papered hunch
  Of mailéd matter thunderous thick,
With Edvard S's quite a bunch,—
  Here, *bearer*, scissors, '*juldi*,' quick!—
Excuse my suave seraphic smile
These happenings please a bibliophile.

Three solid volumes from the sky!
  Prodigious dose of dazzling joy—
Within whose drab dressed covers lie
  Potential bliss, my *bearer* boy!
Church? No! for what are fretted aisles
To fellowship with bibliophiles.

So take the dogs and tie them loose
  Against the north verandah rail,—
And don't let Dooma act the goose
  Nor Loona echo Llama's wail.
And, '*mehta*,' sweep this stuff away—
The ravished wrappings of a day.

This cover,—good—, of chastened grace,
  No goggled motor-maniac loud
Nor girl with *chiffon* hatted face
  Gape grinning for the book-stall crowd).
They loved this very sort of one
When Warrington and Pen were young.

When Ratbolt, Pictor, and Loslein
  The "Kalendarium" did provide
They little thought their front design
  Would deck I. Kobel's neat outside;
And Kobel (Iakob) little knew
The Pearsworth firm would bone it too.

I like the scroll-work interlaced,
  The roundel in the headrule,—thus
The midribbed foliage deftly placed,
  The vase as of Poliphilus.
The "Opus Spericum" to me
Proves Ratbolt was no dolt, not he.

Here're Austin Dobson, Shaw and Crane,
  With Chesterton of worth and weight;
In "Woodcut Rhymes" we meet again
  The "Northwind" of far boyhood's date.
And that one block "Petunia"
Is worth a mint's '*pecunia.*'

Look! verses (Wilde's) of Paduan rule,
  And printed "pourtraicture" galore,
With cartoons rude of Gillray's school,
  And book-plates of "la Pompadour,"
With Raleigh frilled and Shackspeare frillier,
Plus Achilles and Penthesilea.

Then *bearer*, get you gone from sight,—
  But feed the dogs, or else they'll fret 'em,
And close the '*jhilmils*' to the light,
  And put '*cheroots*' where I can get 'em!
The '*dâk*' to-day's both sweet and strong
So call me with the dinner gong!

The Journal, 26*th December* 1909.

THE WAITING WATCHER.

(16*th February* 1910.)

"Mr. Chamberlain took the oath in the Commons to-day, painfully and with difficulty. He was extremely weak. Still assisted he shook hands with the Speaker, using his left hand and went from the House amid absolute silence. General sympathy was felt for him."—Reuter.

THERE'S a good grey Pile with a stream beside it,
  A royal river to lap the Pile,
A kingdom moved with a mob to guide it—
  A-stir to the deep of the heart awhile.

From the wear of a week of wild endeavour
The winners losers, the lost well won,
To the great grey Pile by the regal river
Came men called clear—for the fight was done.

Thither came they from the reek of the striving—
Flushed from the fray, by the torn town tossed,
By the shook shire chose, at the Pile arriving.
Men of the Moment, whatever the cost.

Drawn from the din to the Pile's calm wooing,
Age at the winter and youth at the spring,
Vantaged, exultant, wide voiced to the doing—
Men with a mandate for country and King.

To the palaced porch where the doves are shining,
The statued pave of the Red Lord's hall,
By mullioned panel with pictured lining
Aglow with the gold of the frescoed wall.

Age to the learning, the rest as we find them,
Heirs to the ages of ruling untold,
Parliament men with the Islands behind them—
Kingdom'd of conquest to have and to hold.

Back to the Chamber oft harped to his calling,
Witched to his wiling, and thaned by his art,
Came he, in silence of shadow down falling
Strengthless, the Chieftain, all dauntless at heart.

Youth to the learning, sad age to the knowing,
Labouring, led, where he wrought at their side;
Silent they greet him in sunset's soft glowing
Silent they speed him with God as his guide.

There's a fair grey Pile to the land's love nearest,
There are true hearts beating within the Pile,
There's a waiting watcher to England dearest
And a good God helming the world the while.

The Journal, 27th February 1910.

SIX BOOKS.

SIX books to read at leisure
(A paper-backed sextette)
I've scanned them all with pleasure
And closed them with regret.

" Black Sheep," by Hyatt (Laurie),
  Bids high for loud applause,
'Twill lure from work and worry
  With Ba Ba brebis noirs.

" Sealed Orders "—Carey (Greening),
  A blend of mirth and grief,
Moves with a mystic leaning
  To laughter and relief.

" Man of the Moors " (worth weighted)
  (F. Unwin) comes this way—
By Sutcliffe who narrated
  " A Tragedy in Grey."

" The Marriage of Lord Verriner,"
By Mrs. Grant (Colquhoun)
(John Long) to just the very Her
  Will wile an afternoon.

" The Caxborough Scandal's" spicy,
  By Wishaw told quite well,
And Lucas Cleeve enticy
  With " Lady Susan." (Bell).

From " Reviews of Books."

The Englishman, 7th March 1910

THE GATES OF IND.*

A Gate of Ind is gleaming where the level land lies high
  Along the shining ripples and the palms above the spray,
(By Saugor, with the Sundarbans dune crested sheltered by)—
  The dancing dappled shallows at the ending of the Bay.

The Gates of Ind are sleeping, for the drawn towns skirt the seas
  At rest along the silting of the lone Carnatic shore;
Ah me! the wild of wailing on the wasting of the breeze—
  The thunder echoes rolling from the dun dead fields of war!

---

* From a review of "The Gates of India" by Colonel Sir Thomas Holdich, K.C.M.G., K.C.I.E., C.B., &c.

A Gate of Ind has greeting for the users by the stars
Where the *ghauted* kingdom'd Island calls across the traffic'd foam:
And a Gate of Ind is glowing by the surf fed desert bars
Of Karachi, waiting westward for the legions that will come.

All these be Gates sea-guarded, all the portals of the brine,
They ope along the lapping of the lazy lurking tide,—
The forted fronting thresholds where the English banners shine
To sea-ward, and armadas of a world's keeled comers ride.

But Ind has Gates to landward, looking landward from the gloom,
Time-torn by stroke of tempest, tear-dimmed by blast of dread,—
Towered passes frowned portentous on the battle worlds of doom,
Where the groaning of the ages moans the dirging of the dead.

There are spectral hordes a-passing from the Helmund to Lahore,
And a phantom phalanx fighting where the Khaiber keys the plain,
Where up-stand the granite Gateways, where is broke the shock of war,
And the might of England musters at the porticoes of pain.

The Englishman, 14*th March* 1910.

DISCHARGED.*

(TO THE GUN THAT WENT OFF.)

"'The 9-30 night gun, which has for generations been the signal for the commencement of entertainments, is now a thing of the past. Curious as it may seem, Sir Guy Fleetwood Wilson, 'our Finance Minister,' is held to be responsible for this."—The *Englishman*, 8th April 1910.

CRISP cannonader of the night—
Sharp shudderer of the district daily—
You're "off" at last, and now its quite
A case of "Vale!"

You shot the way around the Clock,
And blustered as you didn't oughter,
Soothsayer of the short, sharp, shock
And smart reporter.

---

* The order to discontinue the firing of the gun (if ever made) was subsequently, to the satisfaction of everybody (Dâk included), countermanded.

And so you're one with them that was
O shivering, shattering, clattering, tartar!
Ta-ta! we'll not regret you 'cause
A rude ramparter—

You made us jump, you made us start—
Just as the night was slowing stilly—
You went and over-did the part
A great big silly.

"The Play's the Thing"! and so you thought
To raise the curtain with a smacker
That shook the town and eke the fort—
Colossal cracker!

You always lacked a sense of what
The papers call "proportion," certain—
It doesn't need a cannon shot
To lift a curtain.

It is not every one who goes
In black and white (the ladies finer)
To decorate our theatre rows—
A half-past-niner.

It isn't every night we look
At stage-land as a sort of heaven,—
It isn't every day we book
With Mister Bevan.

For there are some who take the ground
A gun should turn to better uses,
When *Khitmutghars* are walking round
With green *Chartreuses*.

When "port's the thing!" (and not reports)
Your dinner-din's a trifle jokeless,
It spoils *cheroots* the best of sorts,
All-be-it smokeless.

For they who sit at table late
To puff the weed and tittle-tattle
Can't really quite appreciate
Your smashing rattle.

And so be-gone, big gun,—good-bye
On your discharge we long have puzzled—
And only hope that dear Sir Guy
Will keep you muzzled.

The Journal, 10*th April* 1910.

THE SISTRUM.*

SEB to sire and Nut to mother
Isis and Osiris rise—
Sister-wife and husband-brother
Wombed and wove of Earth and Skies.
Set the smiter, slain of Horus,
Amen-Ra with moon of gold,
Hawk and Bull come by before us—
From the underworld of old.

Hear the rodded sistrum whining
From the Nome of Iquertet,
Chanting An and Iah shining,
Nephthys, spouse of Tebha-set.
Thoth and Sebek, Tum still hearted,
Khu of the Uazit Eye,
Opalled Amentit flood guarded—
Looped with lapis lazuli

Men with gods in seasons sharing
Horizon the wild of Kem,
Gods the Uraeus wearing
Strike the syren sistrum stem.
Gods, disc-crowned, in peaceful meeting
Twice exalt the godlet Hu,—
Heirs of Seb the silence greeting—
Living souls of Istennu

Excellent, the sistrum shaken
Moves to music Luxor fane,
Lures the Pyramids forsaken
So the Pharaohs flame again.
Water-girdled Philae slumbers
Corridored with shades untold
While the braided-sistrum number
Point the liturgies of old.

---

* From a review of "The Burden of Isis" by J. T. Dennis.

Lo, the Maardet boat abiding,
Heb sonorous, loud of lays,
Isis and Osiris gliding
Cavalcade to ope the ways.
Odoured sweet in radiance smiling
Templed Deb unveiléd stands
When the sistrum, bronze, beguiling
Wakes awhile the lotus lands.

The Englishman, 11*th April* 1910.

CHARLES GEORGE HILLERSDEN ALLEN, I.C.S.

Chairman of the Corporation of Calcutta. Born in Leicestershire 1864. Died at Darjeeling, 13th April, 1910.

QUENCHED the torch and void the glass—
Silence, let his spirit pass.
Strength and wisdom, courage high
His were these. And now good-bye.
For a while we knew his sway—
Then the Reaper came this way
Beckoned to the worker true
So he went beyond the view.
So his spirit broke the bars
Where the mountains strike the stars;—

So he sleeps of mortal dust
Nearest to the heights in trust—
Trust that when the Judgment call
Rolls along the mountain wall
And the angel trumpet speaks
Loud o'er the Himalyan peaks,
When the scrolls of fate unfurled
Flame the roof of all the world
And the faithful throng the skies
He with them to God will rise.
His the gain—the losers we
Miserere Domine!

The Journal, 17*th April* 1910.

AB URBE CONDITA.

"I last week named Samuel Oldham as the earliest Bengal undertaker. (See Bengal Obituary, p. 75; and Busteed, p. 172). He is supposed to have taken the marble used for his tombstones from the ruins of Gour. Most of his work was placed in the old burial ground surrounding St. John's Church, and some of it may still be recognised by the initials on the slabs 'S. O. F.' ('Samuel Oldham fecit.') He died in November, 1788, and is buried in South Park Street Cemetery."—From "What we hear" by Dâk in the *Journal*.

BENEATH this stone for all to see
  Lies Samuel Oldham, (*R.I.P.*)
Who chipped his way and chiselled verse
  On chiselled marble (which was worse).
(For truth to say, S.O. was oh so
  So overlax, so very so-so).
His slabs (he sold 'em when he'd stoled 'em)
  Soon filled the ground (it couldn't 'old 'em).
He cut to deal, and shuffled sadly.
  Fate dealt a cut, and hurt him badly.
To S.O. (F.) one ought to soften—
  He didn't go a-gleaning often.
And Fate's insinuating fist
  Who dare defy? Who can resist?

In carving stones for other folk
  He very soon was stony-broke;
A slump set in of polished block
  And polished off his slabs in stock.
It does not fall to everyone
  To crave for bread and ask a stone;
It must have been a case of dread
  To lack a stone to carve for bread.
And so, in an unguarded hour,
  The tempter whispered "go to Gour,—"
"We shouldn't take what isn't ours"
  "Unless we're sure its only Gour's,—"
"There's heaps of marble loot on tap"
  "So go, annex the lot, (*verb. sap.*)."

The cutter, cut off bread and butter,
  Cut off and came back to Calcutta—
On Fate's decrees he'd had revenge
  By scooping in an old Stonehenge.
He'd thought of going on the large
  And mopping up the Agra Taj,

But didn't press the undertaking—
The distance was too aggravating;
And some suggested hide and sneakery
Amid the walls of Futipur Sikri—
"*Phut!* a poor plan!" cried Sam, "too far,"—
"Do hurry up that E. I. R.!"
He rose to fame and worth and pelf,
(The skies help him who helps himself)—
And he who takes what isn't his
Oft murmurs to himself "good biz"—
"Bespoken orders prompt obeyed!"
(Since there are tricks in every trade.)

And, rightly, every one who died
Expected slabs to be supplied—
To blame them is of words a waste—
One must conform to proper taste.
His undertaking overtaken
Old Oldham saved his old old bacon
Lived on,—the pink of high morality—
A local leading "Old Mortality."
None ever deemed his conduct shabby
Whose tombstones were so sleek and slabby,
And none to him cold shoulder turned
Whose increment on urns was earned.

For hatchments he'd attachments bland,
Of hearse and verse a stock to hand,
When for the dead a search you bent
He always knew the mon you meant,
And when you asked for more "lo, see 'em!"
Said he of many a *mausoleum*.
His show-yard was in Coseitollah,
His motto—"next please who's to foller?"
This undertaker undertook
A *trade-de-luxe*—to only book
The cream of them who of their kind
On going left a name behind;
(So when men mentioned his *emporium*
They dubbed it "Oldham's *cre(a)matorium*.")
Who only, in or out of vaults,
Were weighted with but trivial faults—
Mere little slips and slides confessed
(*Humanum* (*um!*) *errare est*.)

He never let a chisel-stroke
  Immortalize the sinful folk—
For, such his nicety of mood,
  He only slabbed the great and good.
His clients were the good and great,
  (He said they were at any rate).
" Memorialize the rest," he cried,
  " I couldn't do it if I tried !"
He said this with an air of squirm—
  (The jobs went to some other firm).

If text or phrase his fancy caught on
  He carved it deep " *Gnothi seauton.*"
" *Hic jacet Dives*, ne'er a betterer "—
  (With torches upside down, *et cetera*).
" *Hinc illæ lachrymæ!*" (that's sobbery)
  " *Semper fidelis—bobberi! bobberi!*"
" *Vixit* (he lived) *apud Lal Dighee.*"
  " All on the square, *bus! vale!*" (*twiggez?*)
And when his whim waxed rather flighty
  He used to add " *Mors phatuk vitæ.*"
Mortuus est—a vir virorum."
  (Where will the Board now find a *quorum?*)
Each babe a beauty (kissy-kissy-ma !)
  Each wife an " *uxor delectissima.*"
His pyramids he'd tier and tier 'em.
  (" *O tempus fugit—edax rerum!*)"
He told us what we ought to do—
  Satis verborum, voila tout, Memento mori je suis prét
Lex script' ab urbe condita.

So there they are before our eyes
In avenues—the brave, the wise,
  In rectitude all gone before,
Qui mal-y-pense, and *honi soit.*
  (I hope that *honi* felt remorse—
To sware is really rather coarse—
  In any cemetery extensive
You're safe to see a *malli* pensive,
  Likewise you'll also find that he
Is often furnished with a key).

His calligraphic art so neat
Last flourished in South Park-e-Street,
And he (*ars longa vita brevis !*)
Is booked by Busteed in a crevice.
Kind reader, ponder, shed a pref-
erential sigh for S.O. (F).

The Journal, *24th April* 1910.

ON AN EDITOR'S LEADER.

"The question is whether Lord Kitchener's genius is of the Wellingtonian or the Napoleonic order. He has certainly never yet failed in any task he has undertaken. We can only trust that, whether he comes back to India or not, he may not be fated to find his Waterloo at Government House."—*The Empire*, 27th May 1910.

ECCENTRIC finis to an *Empire's* say,
Erratic climax, Delphic, yet emphatic ;
I've read it, upside down and every way—
Its enigmatic.

"We only trust that whether he comes back
To Ind or not, that he may not be fated
To find his Waterloo here" (lose the track)
That's stated.

A gentle trust, as proper as correct.
For "K. of K." we've all a love platonic,
And wouldn't like to see his prospects wrecked
Napoleonic.

Its put a trifle lame (as with a wink).
"If he comes back or not." "Or not"'s what gets me.
But there it is in lynotypic ink—
That's what upsets me.

Should he come back or not. It reads so queer—
For if he doesn't chance to top the *guddi*
Where Waterloo comes in is far from clear—
Its muddy.

What's wrong with Waterloo too ? That great name
Is writ in uncials in our Island history—
Linked with Duke Arthur's iron colossal fame.
Here's mystery !

Of all the fights Duke Wellington was at,
Of all his endless tale of glorious tussles,
Why every school-boy knows the best was that
Near Brussels.

To dread lest Kitchener, F. M. should find,
His Waterloo quite close to Thacker Spinks's—
Is riddle cryptic, judgment izing blind,
Smacking of Sphinxes.

Who doubts the genius of great "K. of K."
Is Wellingtonian when all's said and done ?
Who doubts but if he comes he'll come to stay ?
Not I for one.

It's hard to understand the '*Empire's*' trust
That if he don't come back he'll miss the Duke's luck—
And missing turn his big career to dust,
And go and chuck.

It isn't seemly to be so profound.
His leaders usually are unsophistic,—
This latest looked at round and round and round
's superbly mystic.

He writes about the good in everything,
The rare, the right, the real, the ripe, the rotten,—
On Mr. Rooseveldt, or George the King,
Or Evan Cotton.

Propounding now charades on "K" to shock
On sultry afternoons, and fog the cits
In fogs of leaders qualified to knock
Their wits to bits.

He squeals Cassandra-like, to scare the street
The waning glory of our Chieftain's star—
By fearing lest at Government House he meet
His Quatre Bras.

I think I take his meaning, all the same,
Though what he said and meant to say don't tally.
Suppose we let the comet bear the blame
Or Halley !

27th May 1910.

TO THAT INSECT.

" Berlin telegrams report that the Crown Prince is signing the State Papers for the Emperor, whose wrist is badly swollen by the bite of an insect."—*Reuter*, 28*th May* 1910.

ANOPHELES (*proboscis* red),
(Lat :\ " *Musca* ") fine and fat,
" A cat may face a king," 'tis said,
But then you're not a cat.

Will nothing teach you to be wise—
Will nothing make you wiser ?
O, bloatedest of blatant flies—
You've been and bit the Kaiser.

Teutonic trifler, shrill and sly,
Debased Germanic germ,
The worm may tempt the curly fly,—
Though William's not a worm.

The " Yellow Peril " 's now "taboo,"
His roar is like a lamb's ;
He's ceased to plank his revenue
On tanner telegrams.

The only failing that he's got
'S a simple " Dreadnought " fad;
Most kings would cultivate a lot,—
He's really not so bad.

You've frustrated the sports of kings,
Incurred the mailéd fist ;—
You'll pay for with all sorts of things
That badly swollen wrist.

Your wings and stings aint strong enough
To see this trouble through.
To flout a Kaiser in a huff
Is more than you can do.

He's stacks of forts with *glacis* deep
By dynamiters mined,
And spies who never go to sleep—
The secret service kind.

Next time you wind your sultry horn
In merry murderous mood
You'll quite regret that you were born,—
They're safe to tap your blood.

For you've had his, of armèd host
War Lord, and he won't fail
To serve your lithe loose limbs on toast
With salt upon your tail.

The Crown Prince is a-signing hard
State '*chits*' to rear and van
Of horse, police and body-guard
To catch you if they can.

The bitten bites, bear that in mind,
Germania's steely heel
Is up against you, pledged to grind
E'en flies upon a wheel.

A million men, or thereabout,
With Nordenfeldt and lance
Will leap to clutch you by the snout;—
You haven't half a chance.

A million more their nights will spend
And all their afternoons
A-chasing you, my little friend,
In Zeppelin balloons.

Your punishment is great, but then,
It's also only fit,—
The fly that bites the Kaiser men
Has got to pay for it.

All Europe's linked in friendly laws,
It won't avail to seek
The aid in your unhallowed cause
Of *Corps Diplomatique*.

The *Status Quo* for fly or Pope
Must not be risked to-day;—
Don't entertain the slightest hope
Of getting clean away.

28th May, 1910.

A SEXTETTE.

SIX books for glad perusal through a lazy loafing day
On a gliding steamer chunking down a leafy waterway.

"Storm and Treasure" (Methuen)—Bailey—tends to make the eye-lids wet,
Tells of Lucille and the ladder and the "wonder-white" Yvette.

Claire de Pratz (Mills Boon)'s álluring with a winsome witching queen
In "The (Frenchy) Education of (the dainty) Jacqueline."

(Bell). "Pilgrimage of Youth," by D. G. Peto has a yacht
Swamped shoreward near Morocco, you may like it or may not.

Miss Warden—Florence—(Laurie) in her old compelling style
In "Miss Ferriby's Clients" keeps one happy for a while.

"Gilt and Gold" by Jessie Challcombe ("Leisure Hour") 's all pews and peace;
And in "Troubled Waters" Headon Hill's sensations never cease.

The six are full of frivol, fun, fire, fallacies and fac's
Miss Warden's bound in boards (green glazed) the rest have paper backs.

The Englishman, *6th June* 1910.

From "Reviews of Books."

OMIMOSA SAN.

When a Japanese girl dances you see plum-trees, and birds with beaks, starry nights, pagodas, cherry petals, gold fish, dragons of a light soft green colour, frogs, figs, ivory buttons, parasols, volcanoes, damask kites, and welshrabbits.

THERE are things that you never conceived of before
In Amé-no-Uzumé's *repertoire*.
There are cloudlets afloat and a wakayama
That bubbles about to a fixed formula;
A mystical measure
For popular pleasure
To lure into love and ecstaticise leisure;

From a Review of "The Japanese Dance" by Marcelle A. Hinks.

Imayo lutes, songs,
Gold umbrellas and gongs,—
And tortoise-shell devils with red lacquer prongs,
And cinnamon mimes
Up to all sorts of gimes,
(One can't always hit on the right kind of rhymes).
A Geisha's a flirt
In a blue rumpled skirt
As nippy as ninepins and twice as alert;
And Ameterasu
A Goddess who casu-
  ally comes down and then afterwards has you,
While eight million godlings smile sailing around
On mats where tarantella spiders abound,
In masks made of lac,
With a comb at the back,
And scarlet *kimonos* uncommonly slack.
These things that you'd never conceive could exist
Are in Amé-no-Uzumé's "properties" list—
For dramas that go on for weeks at a time
Run by acrocrobatic or bucolic mime—
Cloak for beautiful metaphors, similes dread,
Till you creep away home with a pain in the head
To wake in the morn with your nose on the floor
And remark "Amé-no-Uzumé never no more
Will I cultivate classical, assical lore!"
Your Shinto arenas,
Slit-eyed *contadinas*,
And sleeve-wagging, toe-dragging, prim *ballerinas*—
Are all very well for Hiogo or Tokio
But for me the're no go, or put briefly no jokio!

The Englishman, *27th June* 1910.

THE DAUNTLESS THREE.

I glanced from the verandah rail
  Upon the tennis ground—
Where head aloft, and curl on tail,
  The dogs were roving round.

Sleek Dooma, furred in silken grace,
  And Llama of renown,
With Loona of the loving face—
  The best of dogs in town.

The lawn to them was green and sweet,
  A walled and gated home,
And nought to them the dusty street
  Where goats and cattle roam.

Came someone's dog, a burly chow,
  With nose and crest elate—
A gentleman—but anyhow
  They drove him through the gate.

And next a cat, a decent sort,
  All pepper, spurs and spits,
They chased her round the tennis court
  And barked themselves to bits.

(A cat upon a wall out late
  Don't matter, not at all,
It's not the cat or wall you hate,
  It's just the caterwaul.)

A squirrel with his plume a-tuft
  Hopped by, they let him pass,
Then lay upon their backs and "woughed"
  And rolled upon the grass.

They forced a crowd of crows to quit,
  —A chattering clattering crew,—
Then rambled round the world a-bit
  For something else to do.

Until two *bandars* from a tree
  Dropped down with shriek and squall,
And shouting at the dauntless three,
  Sat jabbering on a wall.

The dauntless three on halting paw
  Drew close with care astute,
They'd never seen that sort before
  And didn't like the brute.

The monkeys groaned and laughed and wept,
  And wagged their arms in air,
The dauntless three together crept
    To diagnose the pair.

They didn't bark, they gazed in scorn,
  A deep disgusted three,
Then backed across the tennis lawn
  And clambered up to me.

L 7

Thence from the wide verandah high
  Well shielded from the foe,
While I was by, the three let fly
  And let their feelings go.

They barked their minds on monkeys black
  Each brother, son, and bride,
For fourteen generations back
  Upon the uncle's side.

It did them good to let off steam
  In reckless wrath all hot.
  * * * * *
I left them fast asleep to dream
  Each curled up in a knot.

Wise dogs, thought I, to clear away
  From venomed rogues a-row,—
You'll live to bark another day
  If you back out and go.

A decent dog is ne'er afraid
  To back from poisoned stab,
His pretty throat was never made
  For monkey claws to grab.

Until you're safe don't even growl
  Whatever may befall,
And always back when *bandars* prowl
  And leave them on the wall.

2nd July, 1910.

THE SCENT OF THE ROSES.

An autobiography full of picturesque and varying interest frankly told. The Princess' idea of the Art of Life has been "to enjoy to the full the scent of the roses and all other gifts of nature, while carefully avoiding the thorns."

SWEET scent of the roses, the roses awaking,
  The red petalled roses, the dew on them wet,
It comes to the heal of the heart that is aching
The rose-scent of morning to chasten regret.

Oh, scent of the roses, the roses a-weeping,
  The fire-fashioned roses a-flame to the last,
A-waft to the soul of the sin that is sleeping
  The sin of the sunless when daylight is past.

Sharp thorn of the roses a-sib to the sinning,
  The thorn thoughted roses, the blood on them yet,
The flail of the loss that is holden the winning,
  The moan of the mourning to them that forget.

Oh, thorn of the roses, the thorn that is slaying
  The garlanded roses, a canker at heart,
It stabs where the red-nodding roses are straying,
  It slays where the tears of the late lovers start.

Sad scent of the roses, the roses decaying,
  The thorn wasted roses of sin and of sigh,
Sad thorn of the roses, the lovers' dismaying—
  The love for a day is the love that will die.

Songed scent of the rose, of the roses a-shining,
  The red centred roses with joy over-cast;
Now pluckt is the thorn of the lover's repining—
  "The love for a life is the love that will last!"

From a review of "Princess Helene Von Recowitza," an autobiography.

The Englishman, 11th July 1910.

AT CHOTA HAZRI.

"The memorial to Edward VII must be local and imperial, useful and ornamental, representative of all and the servant of all. The first proposal that occurs to us, is the suggestion made by "Dak," long before the conference was thought of. "Dak's" idea is the most magnificent. It is based on the memorial to Victoria, which is to be augmented by a garden, statues, and processional way."—*The Journal, 24th July* 1910.

I like to read of Savarkar, his sprint at gay Marseilles;
  Of Johnson and of Jeffries at Nevada, "hard as nails;"
Of Liabeuf, the guillotined, the Paris Apache,
And other folk who grace the news with tea and toast to-day.

I like to read of flying men, the more or less insane;
Of Lady Abdy "crazy" for a channel aeroplane;
But best to read the "Hostel scheme"* is only "in the air"
Now Sir Edward's been explaining to Sir Lawrence in the chair.

But while I peel a plantain, while I stir a cup of tea,
A horrid thought arises which it's quite perplexing me,
The thought of that sad morrow, oh it makes my spirit ache,
When people cease suggesting just the form the thing should take.

I like to read the papers, my patriot spirit beams;
I like to read of people with a lot of different schemes;
King Edward's dead, that's certain, but it isn't quite as clear
Just what Sir Edward wanted when he spoke at Belvedere.

But that's just where the fun comes in, the fat's on fire (what ho!)
Now we all of us are happy till the 5th of proximo;
We'll all make scheme suggestions in the sweetest, suavest way
And can calculate (*pro rata*) on a crop of nine a day.

But still I'm far from placid, for I look a lot ahead,
To a closed suggestion season when suggestion time is dead;
When packed waste-paper baskets range in rows upon the stair
And we read no more of meetings with Sir Lawrence in the chair.

So let's be up and doing while to-day is yet to face,
Shame the stars of morning singing while they roll about in space;
Get stylos by the dozen, and buy foolscap at the ream;
Cram steam, turn tap,—'suggestions for the King's Memorial Scheme!'

The Journal, *24th July* 1910.

THE NON-MELANCHOLY DANE.

"Sir Louis Dane during his recent visit to Delhi has visited the various sites suggested for the All India Memorial to the late King Emperor and has cheerfully inspected the improvements carried out in the Fort gardens and drainage system."—*The Englishman*, *29th July* 1910.

SIR Louis Dane, Sir Louis Dane
(They'd all at-once improved a drain)
Walked cheerfully for miles and miles
Sans smells, returning smiles for smiles.

*** Sir Edward Baker, Lieutenant-Governor of Bengal, at one time had desired that the Memorial should take the form of a Hostel for Indian students. His proposal met with strong and successful opposition.**

He beamed upon the Chandni Chowk
  And thought the *ekkas* quite a joke;
Though when he reached the Kashmir Gate
  His mirth, restrained, grew less elate.

The Mosque of haughty Humayoon
  Quite cheered him up all afternoon,
And meeting with the Musjid yellow
  His joy approached the ultra-mellow.

The Kutub, climbing to the sky
  Increased his risability;—
So striking on a statue site
  He laughed and laughed in sheer delight.

And when they showed him others various
  Sir Louis grew quite Loui(s) larious.
And when they said they wanted money
  He chuckled "do you? don't be funny!"

Sir Louis Dane, Sir Louis Dane,
  (They'd cheerfully improved a drain)—
Both viewed the Fort and Gardens system—
  And cried to think he might have missed 'em.

31*st July* 1910.

A MAN'S HATE.*

COME if thou cans't, some uglier raging hide,
  My hate pretends not that I'm going there,
It is mine own and never can't abide
  Be I most close reproved, or be thou clear.
    But hate, thou must not crow—
      I will be false!

Change for a dib—three annas—and no less—
  Our hate forfendeth it upon my word,
It won't be mine—quite as it's not—confess
  Because we fought and always overheard.
    But hate, it's all no go,
      I must be false!

* (The pages of the "Journal" had been for some time open to verse by lady writers whose muse tended towards the doleful. This monstrosity is a parody of Woman's Love" that had graced the paper a week previously.)

Squeak as thou may'st in bold or slender groan,
My hate, loathed too, perturbs not on thy screech,—
Since it was stolen, mine it is, a loan
Unlent to me, to stick to like a leech.
But hate, O, dear me, O
I shall be false!

Fact as it's not—be blind—or be my foe,
My hate suspends itself and nothing heeds,
It is a shift, my hate, I would not owe—
It's jolly fine on whatsoe'er it feeds.
But hate, how coulds't thou know?
I've jolly well got to be false!

Hate whom I won't, don't ask it not of me,
My hate hates so perpending on it quite,
(I'm off the hooks a bit but wait and see
With luck I'll fake and fake the metre right).
But fate, 'twas never so—
That I am false.

Burn if thou dare'st this screed, it's quite at sea
Ah hated one, my hate is all uncaught,
It "taketh nought," it don't, no thanks to thee—
And "asketh which" where it was never sought.
Yes, hate, likewise "what ho"—
I really am going to be false!

The Journal, 31st July 1910.

THE PUNCH CARTOONS.

PENCILLINGS proud with memories gleaming,
Good, gay, streaming
In full flow,
Eloquent artistry deftly dreaming
Dimly out of the dead days glow.

Old time odours about them clinging,
Bell-calls ringing
Lost chimes clear,
Clanging of sad sweet things rebringing
Glamour of deeds of the old days dear.

Delicate tracery, charm compelling,
Wisdom welling,
Lifting the heart—
Conquering resonance, echoing, telling
Of bosom throbbed when the tear-drops start.

Pencillings, stencillings, laughing, weeping,
Crowding, creeping,
Loyal and leal;
Time kissed treasures of stately reaping,—
Shadowy sheddings of Time's appeal.

The Journal, 7th August 1910.

A QUARTETTE.

"Vocation." By Lily Grant Duff. Murray's Imperial Library.

THE location of "Vocation" isn't difficult to place,
It gets at you, it holds you, and it hits you in the face.
It's all about a "Gordon Rex" whose portrait, so they tell
Was painted for "the Salon" by "Cette petite demoiselle."

"How she played the Game." By Lady Napier of Magdala. Murray's Imperial Library.

And this is "how she played the game" when standing on the stair
To greet her crowd of ducal guests, gem-crowned in red-gold hair,
"How sweet you look!" said Lady Price (aside) "The horrid cat!"
"Your tiara is crooked, dear!" said Jean.—("She's getting fat!")

"Jewell," by Clara Louise Burnham in Constable's Sixpenny Series.

"Sing once again the song you sang!" (the stars were shining wide),
And she began to softly sing close nestled to his side.
"From tired joy and grief afar and ever nearer Thee,—"
"Father, where thine own children are I ever love to be!"

"The Success of Mark Wyngate." By Una L. Silberrad in Constable's Sixpenny Series.

Mark did not hear, the twilight filled the silence of the room,
In darkness then a toddling child came feeling through the gloom,
"Is fraulein's work quite finished?" asked the little one and smiled,
"She's resting now for ever!" said the man, and kissed the child.

From "Reviews of Books."

The Englishman, 15th August 1910.

"A BACK WORD."

Mr. Rudyard Kipling's Suggestion.

"Mr. Rudyard Kipling has been considering the advisability of adopting some scheme for protecting an airman against a fall. The resnlt of his consideration is embodied in a letter illustrated by diagrams, which appears in this week's *Car*.

"'As far as I can make out,' he says, 'men go up with less protection, than is worn by the catcher of a baseball team.'

"'I suggest a helmet of rubber inflated on the crown of the head, and round the back and over the collar bones. What you want is the protection of the neck against a backward or forward wrench. The height of the padding on the addahdcehrad daoshr dllaofd raohtraf dwofdoc mra mfwl tato inoh ohrdl dodw etahid rlufysh Knt lost6nt8 inHH efi S gzo.'"—*The Englishman, 16th August*, 1910.

TWINKLE, twinkle, little Car
Kipling catch and there you are,
Up above the world so high
With the fly-men in the sky.

Beautiful *Car* from heaven so bright
Softly falls protected wight
When he falleth to earth afar
Car of the Kipling, beautiful *Car*.

When the padding height is known
Kipling's prose seems too high flown—
Kiplingesque his latest's quite
Kipling, Kipling, out of sight.

17*th August* 1910.

POT POURRI.

"Mrs. Wilmot Corfield's Entertainment."

"Mrs. Wilmot Corfield, who organised the entertainment in aid of St. Paul's Children's Home, Scott's Lane, Calcutta, given at the Empire Theatre last night, has good reason, as also have the managers of the Home, to be satisfied with the result of her labours, for there was hardly a seat vacant in the huge theatre, and the result should be the handing over of a substantial cheque for the Home. The immense audience, too, seemed delighted with the entertainment and rapturously applauded everything, which again must have been very satisfactory to Mrs. Corfield, as well as to the ladies and gentlemen who so generously gave their services."

The above is from a report in the *Statesman* of a "Pot-pourri" entertainment under the Patronage of Their Excellencies the Viceroy and the Countess of Minto, C.I.; His Honor Sir Edward Baker, K.C.S.I., Lieutenant-Governor of Bengal; Sir Lawrence Jenkins, K.C.I.E., Chief Justice of Bengal; and Colonel Shute and the Officers of the Rifle Brigade, given on the 16th August 1910, the financial result of which was eminently satisfactory. The following topical verses with choruses serving as *encores*, were well received, and according to the *Empress* of many days after "survive at bridge parties and such convivial gatherings." Mr. L. May and Mr. E. R. Hartly led the choruses.

(I.)

AWAY! come away from the hill-land
Away! come away from the stew!
When you're safe in Calcutta
The maidan will put a
Fine breeze by the golf-club for you.—
You'll call on the ladies on Sundays,
Then indulge in a dinner (with sweeties),
And smile, as you swear,
There are no girls up there
Like those you may take to Peliti's.

By the shore of the Tollygunge tanklet so blue, blue, blue,
There are maids who love jumping gymkhanas, they do, do, do,
And whenever you like
They will teach you to bike to the Zoo, Zoo, Zoo.
For our girls have a tone of their own be it known, just for you, you, you.

You need never go back to the hill-land
But sit with your quiet cigar.
The smoke rings up-rolling
Your sad thoughts consoling
For those in the fog lands afar.

There are dear little ladies on Sundays
Just fitted for *phitton* or *dinghy*,
With sweet pretty faces
And chiffons and laces
Down Alipore way or Chowringhee.

In the shade of the big Banian branches askew—skew—skew,
(They haven't got anything like it at Kew, Kew, Kew),
She who must be obeyed
Is the only maid made just for you, you, you,
There are girls of the kind, though not easy to find,
For they're few, few, few.

(II.)

The women folk are past a joke,
As Suffragettes they're posing—
No Suffragette a vote will get—
Unless John Bull is dozing;
Mauve, green and white, their colours bright,
A high flown art selection—
To suit the tall, the short, the small,
And each kind of complexion.

Oh, be careful of the Suffragette,
Ask the Crocodile to sight her—
She's getting hoarse and husky
And she makes Mr. Asquith tusky;
Ask her to dinner with the Crocodile—
And very soon he'll delight her—
It's a penny to a pin that the Croc. takes her in—
The poor, deluded Crocodile.

Big buildings high that strike the sky
Around the town are looming—
The Grand Hotel is doing well,
The Empire Theatre's booming;—
But one lost friend has reached an end
We're each and all a mourner,—
So heave a sigh and wipe your eye
For poor Scott Thomson's Corner.

Oh, be careful of the crocodile—
Coax the crocodile to go now—
He's lanky, long, and lucky,
He's feeling tired though plucky.—
Here's to Lord Minto and his lady fair,
We all shall miss them so now,—
But Lord Hardinge he's a brick and he'll be here pretty quick—
Don't let him catch the Crocodile.

Vide also "In as much as" in "Dâk Dicta" (page 90).

16*th August* 1910.

ON ANYTHING.

TAKE hold of the "Post of the Morning"
And stand in the Strand till it's read—
And you'll lay in a stock of the wit of Belloc
"On Anything" out of his head.

From a review of "On Anything" by Mr. H. Belloc.

The Englishman, 22*nd August* 1910.

ADRIFT.

THE sish is deep, the slob packed loose to sinking,
Great chasm dun comes by to cloak and kill,—
Dim gap along the racing landwash blinking—
And ice-pan heaved as stones of Freya's mill.

And still they strive with eager neck out-thrusting,—
Big "Brin" white chieftain of the burly breast,
"Doc" gentle beast of joyous bark full trusting,
Slim "Spy" wise, wiry, with a lion chest.

Then, "Moody," plodder, ne'er behind him glancing,
And "Watch," the speedy, liquid eyes a-glow,
Roan, "Jerry," firm of foot, for aye advancing—
And "Sue," like great grey wolf, an Eskimo.

Last jet black "Jack," the tender true retriever—
Who always runs the first before the sledge,
And never looking back pulls on for ever
To the far rim of purple star-set's edge.

Out of the night, I see them, teaming, dreaming,—
On ever on, none ever look behind,
Into the night they go, for ever streaming—
Gods' ghost-pack scampering with the Spirit's wind.

Then list the gods across the landwash calling,
Though chasm yawn and slob-pan loose to sink,
Thy path is onward to the planet's falling—
Right on to reach the shining star-set's brink.

And when that bright light brink is touched, and turning
Thou see'st the way by thee and dog o'er past,
And know'est the gods went with thee, to thy learning,
And on before the white eternal Vast—

There then shall gleam beyond the star-beams setting
Rich red auroras till the Day-Star glow
For faithful man and gallant dog forgetting
The dead dark nights of striving through the snow.

From a review of "Adrift on an Ice-pan" by N. P. Grenfell.

The Englishman, 22nd August 1910.

AT THE PARLIAMENT HOUSE.*

For the meeting of the Calcutta Parliament on Friday last a "tremendous House" had been confidently predicted by a writer in "Calcutta, Day by Day," in the *Empire*, in consequence of its being the first occasion upon which ladies had had the opportunity of admission to membership. As a matter of fact no lady member attended and only three ladies occupied seats in the visitors' gallery.

O, Woman (while we bend the knees
Uncertain, coy, and hard to please)
For vote and seat you made a vow—
And went and won them, anyhow.

"You shall have both!" the House replied,
"Walk up, walk up, pray come inside!"
"Step in!" said Woolacott, "and sit!"
And Horniman said ditto, dit.

*** At this time "Dâk" was Secretary of State for the Colonies in a Unionist Ministry.**

The *Empire* man (a man of nous)
Predicted "a tremendous House."
The Cabinet of matchless mien
Created an imposing scene.

The Speaker sat, the House was set
To greet each gracious Suffragette;
The Speaker sighed, the House was calm,
White-waistcoated, the mould of form.

The Speaker sat, the Speaker sighed—
And Woolacott the ceiling eyed,
The Speaker sighed and seemed in doubt—
And Horniman glanced round about.

"She cometh not—the hour is past!"
Groaned Premier Horniman at last—
"That clock is fast, it's always so!"
Moaned Woolacott, "and Woman's slow!"

The members gazed across the floor,
No Peri waited at the door,—
No Peri, it must be confessed,
Turned up and meant to do her best.

Then, thus the chair, "Attention pray"
"We'll take the orders of the day,"—
"Though pain and anguish rack the brow,"
"I don't suppose she's coming now."

She didn't come, she smiled beyond
The legislative precincts fond,
And Horniman passed Woolacott
Some stoppered salts upon the spot.

"Buck up" sobbed he, "you're feeling faint!"
And Woolacott snapped "No, I aint!"
(He'd some excuse it seems to me
For this uncivil repartee.)

And both of them are searching far
For him who penned that *Empire* par,
That *Empire* man—a man of nous—
Who scented "Angels in the House."

And each, if caught in pensive way,
Is known to ruminate, they say—
"O Woman—!" (But relate I'll not
What Horniman tells Woolacott.)

The Empire, 31st August 1910.

THACKERAY AND MACAULAY.

The Calcutta Historical Society is taking steps to arrange for the commemoration in 1911 of the centenary of the birth in Calcutta of William Makepeace Thackeray. It is proposed to place a *replica* of Thackeray's bust as a boy,* in the National Portrait Gallery, Trafalgar Square, in St. John's Church, Calcutta, where the novelist was baptised.

THERE was a nice Calcutta boy, with neat and curly hair,
They built a bust about that boy for great Trafalgar Square;
The C. H. S. says "dear me, yes, we really think we must
"Collect the funds, so our St. John's, may boast another bust!"

Lord Curzon's memorial tablet to Thomas Babington Macaulay, which formerly graced a gate-post of his now demolished house in Chowringhee, has recently been replaced upon the outer front wall of the new Bengal Club Building. The inscription has been altered to suit the circumstances.

A house there was that bore a slab to Lord of Lute and Lay,
A knave of clubs did grab that slab and took it clean away;
But, when it saw its house was gone, with all its might and main
It popped into another house and dabbed it on again.

The Empire, 9th September 1910.

*** At a meeting of the Thackeray Centenary Fund Council subsequently held in the Council Chamber of the Asiatic Society of Bengal, "Dak" formally proposed the acquirement of a *replica* of Deville's "boy" bust. His resolution, however, was defeated by the casting vote of the Chairman only and another adopted for the acquirement of a bust of the novelist at mature age. The chairman bore the Thackerayan name of "Dobbin."**

"EENGONYAMA."

"You are not a few boys playing on the maidan, but are known to all the world and have become a recognised and important feature of our vast Empire. Your particular Patrol, I understand, is 'The Service Patrol' and in future you will carry that animal's head upon your flag. Well, we all know what smart clever dogs terriers are, honest, faithful and true, and I am quite certain that if you follow their example you will become a credit to your country."

From a speech by Mrs. Oxenham Menzies to the Boy Scouts when presenting a Flag.—The *Empire*, *6th September* 1910.

I really cannot quite make out
  Just why the lady went and said—
"Here, take this flag, my little scout,"
  "It's decorated with a head."
"If you a Terrier emulate"
  "And wave the beast through thick and thin"
"You'll be a credit to the state."
  (I don't see where the dog comes in.)

A Service head's a sort of chief
  Who rules departments rather well,
(At least this once was my belief—
  I thought he was an awful swell.)
But now they've stuck him on a flag—
  (A fact I've mentioned once before)
For little boys to go and wag
  (I can't think what they've done it for).

7th September 1910.

"QUEEN ANNE'S DEAD."

"The pages of history provide brilliant examples of advancement under female sovereignty. Great Britain dates as a world-power from the reign of Queen Elizabeth. Her arms were then successful both by land and sea, colonies were founded ; art and literature flourished and the people emerged from a state of savagery to civilization. Under good Queen Bess the country experienced another great revival, all along the line, and the benefits of female rule are demonstrated unmistakably by the epoch-making deeds of the Victorian period."—*The Empire*, *6th September* 1910.

WHEN great Eliza filled the throne
  Old England held the world her own.
Then good Queen Bess, by grace divine,
  Went forward, all along the line—
Until Victoria's period crowned
  With epoch-making deeds came round.

* * * * * *

She's dead of course with all her clan,—
But what's the matter with Queen Anne ?

The Journal, 11th September 1910.

HISILLUSIONMENT.

"The *Berliner Zeitung* says: "The Kaiser regards himself as the instrument of the Lord, and will go his way without regard to the views and opinions of the day.

The King's new conception of a state of relation which in no way consorts with modern constitutional ideas will awaken a stormy echo outside Persia. In the component states of the German Empire the bitter hisillusionment which August 26 has brought will be felt not only by the people but by the ruers."—*The Englishman, 12th September* 1910.

THE *Berliner Zeitung* gives tongue, the Kaiser bars inertia,
His new conceptions agitate storm echoes outside Persia.
The ruers will rue ony day that hatched a dis-illusionment,
The people (and perhaps the pope) will hiss his hisillusionment.

12th September 1910.

SWITZERLAND.

I'D like to live in Switzerland and hear the porters yell—
"Next platform for the 5-15 !" "Change here for Neufchatel !"
I'd like to glide in motor-cars above the firs and fogs.
It's nicer far than jogging by on big St. Bernard dogs.

I'd like to climb a mountain steep and feel that at the top
I'm safe to find a telephone and picture-post-card shop.
I'd like to lug my Kodak out from bulky brass bound box
And shoot the chamois balanced high on bits of pointed rocks.

I'd like to look from Lake Lucerne on Zeppelins in flight—
It must be fine to flap around like Mr. Grahame White.
I'd like to live a Switzer free of Kaiser and of Krupp
And feel no German "Dreadnought" means to come and mop me up.

I'd like to skip with mountain goats and antelopes and rams
And form a company to float Mont Blanc Marconigrams.
I'd like to live where glaciers glide and avalanches break
And have a launch (electric mind) to ply the placid lake.

I'd like to wield an alpenstock and wind an Alpine horn
When winding up a cuckoo clock to wake me up at morn.
I'd like to hang head-foremost down and pluck the edelweiss;
But I must stop "I'd liking" now, it's such an idle vice.

The Englishman, 12th September 1910.

AT THE PARLIAMENT HOUSE.

IT met. It sat. A sad sea change pervaded in a crack,
  The party of some forty days had faded in the week;
A Premier into office rode upon the wireless back
  Of a Marconi telegram,—a fine elusive squeak.

I like to picture to myself that high historic scene,—
  That wireless mount, that rider bold agog for power and place,—
That one vote lacking party lost, of proud though puzzled mien,—
  That Premier with a vote too much careering into space.

It met. It sat. The Premier rose and cooed his bill of fare,
  Then named his cabinet, in sooth, a veteran gang the lot,
Whereat a complicated clang of claymores rent the air
  While parties went to war a while and went it strong and hot.

Next purring Peace. The lamb fell fond upon the lion's neck—
  The lion drooped with melting mane upon the other's chest.
They purred round one another's shanks with pert and pretty peck,
  And just because the House agreed Lord Minto did his best.

I like to see the House a-whirl when feathers strew the ground,
  I like to see the mettled hosts galumping out to wars:
But when the mettled hosts as lambs go bleating all around
  Oh, blesséd unanimity! Oh, blessed mettled bores!

In blesséd unanimity the House of fervour fine
  Was pleased to plan to pedestal Lord Minto on a horse.
What only one—one pedestal—oh wherefore draw the line?
  Indent a brace, restore to grace Lord Ripon too, of course!

The Journal, 18th September 1910.

IMPROMPTU AT THE PARLIAMENT HOUSE.

THERE was a man, a *Horny man,*
  And he was wireless wise—
He jumped into a quick-change hedge
  And scratched out all his "ayes."
But when he saw his "ayes" were gone,
  And all his fight in vain,
He jumped upon *Woolly cot*
  And scratched them in again.

23rd September 1910.

THE LITTLE NIPPER UP-TO-DATE.

(With apologies to Mr. Albert Chevalier.)

I'M very near the 'appiest *sahib* about,
I've got a little nipper—'e's a scout—
I'll lay you fifty dibs to two or three
You'd take 'im for a *chota* Baden P.
Now, as for Enery Nooman I've respect,
I thought I'd bring the nipper up correct—
So I says, says I, "Now *dekko* Master Jim
You allus take your little tips from 'im."
And Jim's a Bobs Bahadur,—
Do me proud, but 'e's a Mongoose,
Takes arter one, and aint a bit too tall,—

'E calls the Terriers 'Ooloos';"
And the Curlews "good old Zulus;"
And 'e only stands about so 'igh that's all!

'E gets me on the *maidan* when we're out
And 'e starts away first aidin' of a scout,
To see 'im rub a Tiger—well its great
And it takes a bit o' rubbin' at 'is weight.
'E'll ambulance a Mongoose in 'is boots,
And 'aint 'e just a terror when 'e shoots?
I loves to see 'is flag a waggin' trumps
And 'im shoutin' "eengonyama" as 'e jumps.
There 'e's a Bobs Bahadur,—
Do me proud, but 'e's a Mongoose;
I've knowd 'im wave a bamboo ten feet tall—
'E's perlite to all the lidies,
And saloots Apostolides
And 'e only stands about so 'igh, that's all!

I used to do the Red Road, every night,
The Band or Club and often come 'ome lite,
But now from all such 'abits I've got loosed
And we stalks them flying foxes 'ome to roost.
'E's muggin' up the Scout Law all complete
And 'e 'ates to loaf and can't abide a cheat—
"For Mongooses" says 'e "I 'as my 'opes—"
"But I 'as my doubts about them Antelopes!"

Only last Saturday me an' 'is ayah took 'im out for a walk, I should say 'e took us out. As we was comin' 'ome I says, says I, "lets pop into Castellazzo's," I says, "an' 'ave a cup o' tea" I says. So in I goes follered by 'is Nibs, so I goes to the counter and calls for two of the cup as cheers. "Oh," says 'e, "aint Ayah goin' to 'ave none?"

Oh, 'e's a Bobs Bahadur,—
Do me proud, but 'e's a Mongoose,
Says 'e "its teen peearlers now—my call."
Do me proud, its no *chilakhi*,—
'E's a Baden Powell in *Khaki*—
And 'e only stands about so 'igh that's all!

The Journal, 25th September 1910.

POT POURRI AGAIN.

"Boy Scouts on the Stage."

"Mrs. Wilmot Corfield's Entertainment."

"The Scouts are now an established feature of Calcutta life and under Mr. Newman's guidance are developing daily into a force making for picturesque utility. Last night saw the handsome and spacious Empire Theatre comfortably filled with enthusiastic admirers of the Scouts who very obviously appreciated the untiring efforts of Mrs. Corfield and her artistic band of actors, singers, and musicians to afford Calcutta in *pre-poojah* days an excellent evening's amusement. Their Excellencies Lord and Lady Minto extended their patronage to the entertainment, as also did His Honour Sir Edward Baker, Lady Baker, Colonel Shute of the Rifle Brigade, and Lieutenant-Colonel Apostolides, with a representative committee of well-known ladies and gentlemen. The programme, a bright and attractive one, was (with the exception of a solitary item) entirely new, and its record will live daintily enshrined in the *khaki* covered pages of an illustrated programme specially prepared for the occasion, a model of discreet art and artfulness. "Dâk's" topical verses (as *encores*) went with a swing. The Scouts acquitted themselves gallantly." Miss Alice Gomez was one of the vocalists and Messrs. E. R. Hartley and T. A. Kay led the choruses.

The above is an extract taken from the report of the entertainment of the 27th September 1910, which appeared in the *Englishman* of the following day. The financial result proved more than satisfactory and the topical verses (*encores* to choruses) referred to above were as follows:—

I.

WE'VE been the A. D. S. to see
In one perpetual flow,
We think the "Bal Masqué" immense,
The funniosities intense
Of Zimmerman & Co.
For Zimmerman remains the rage
Of our Imperial local stage.

Vide also "The Song of the Scouts" in "Dâk Dicta" (page 93).

And Goss has made a record gate
  In fine financial groove—
The universal comment's thus—
They'd almost act as well as us
  If only they'd improve.
We'll miss her badly we're afraid
The A. D. S.'s gay "French Maid."

When good Lord Minto ruled the land
  'Neath great King Edward's line
Then all the town was of one mind
To generosity inclined
  And charity divine.
Calcutta proved well up-to-date
At Lady Minto's glorious Fête.

And when Lord Hardinge legislates
  In full viceregal fig
Another Minto Fête we'll plan
To decorate the green maidan
  And do it just as big;—
For charity we'll strive again
In our King George's glorious reign.

II.

The Empire seats rise tier and tier,
The shout o'the scout we hear,
How smart all the lads appear,
In gay patrol that's now so near,
We'll give 'em a hearty cheer as they come by!
  They're stepping light with figure slight
  And these are the boys who come wheeling into sight
In *Khaki* neat with kit complete
And from many an English heart goes up the cry—

Here comes my "Curlew" scout,
My "Tiger-Terrier's" out
  Patrolling from the big *Maidan*,
  What the "Terriers" do the "Curlews" can,
With their "Eengonyama" yell.—
  March, march with bamboo strong,
  Hat slouched, they march along;
They'll make a name in history
And we'll cheer them as we cheer B. P.
They're our own lads marching there.

27th September 1910.

THE POINT OF VIEW.

LISTEN, I've struck Calcutta from a sort
  Of novel coign of vantage newly found.
I overhauled the Empire and I sought
  The circle ultimate that galleries round
      Beneath the dome
Against the ceiling flat; and there at rest
  Leaned, twinkling like an asteroid at home
On all beneath, Calcutta at her best,—
Artistically dined, and most superbly dressed.

Calcutta came, then hovered at the door
  Or trod the neat encircling pavement white,
Paused, midmost, crossing the mosaic floor
  And smiled and laughed and nodded left and right
      To friends she spied,
In prime post-prandial mood. On pleasure set,
  Her dinner done, she to the play-house hied
To cheer the Scouts, or part, to loud regret,
With dainty, dancing, dallying smart Suzette.

Spread out Society aint up to much;
  Its when you strike Society askew
And focussed that you realize that touch
  Which condensation lends the point of view.
      "Good gracious, Oh!"
"What is it?" (so my murmurous musing ran)—
  That smart kaleidoscopic hive below—
Your *burra sahib*—a quite abnormal man,—
Your aunt—a lady mostly feet and fan?

I think it was Diogenes the grey,
  Who sat within a tub and thought a lot
About the people of his paltry day
  And all the funny fussy fads they'd got.
      But bless you, no,
He never scanned Society askew
  In one bright mingled phalanx down below,
Meshed in a magic massed mosaic ring
And impulsed to one mind—"the Play's the thing."

"Man's a forked radish usually an ass"—
  Thus the sad Sage of Chelsea in the dumps—
(Could he have seen that quaint procession pass
  His language would have fizzled out in jumps—
      It really would.)

Calcutta came with tickets, statuesque,
  Enigma'd so you wouldn't if you could
Believe your senses, just at first, grotesque,
Weird, metamorphisised to bland burlesque.

I never met a more facetious crew
  Of ladies fair, and gentlemen as fine,
The which alway depended on the view
  You got, and how and where it drew the line.
          That silly minx—
The point of view is everything. But stop—
  We're cinnamatographed Darwinian links,
Mere marionettes in life's wind-windowed shop
Conspicuous for a lack (or lot) of hair on top.

If so be Art is Beauty,—Beauty Truth,
  Why there you are (thus Mister Bernard Shaw,
And Kipling, Dante, Chesterton, in sooth
  John Milton and about a million more
          Alive and dead,)
Then Art spells Beauty, both together spell
  That Laboucherean lass of whom 'tis said
That she presumably prefers to dwell
And comb her yellow curls at bottom of a well.

If Truth prefers a netherish kind of hole
  It's not for me to worry much about
The means to lift that deep deluded soul,—
  To elevate the Lady—fish her out.—
          What could I do
To lug her to a hygienic flat,—
  To sanitate her mildewed point of view—
To make her wipe her feet upon the mat?
Let well alone! What's Truth? What is she? Answer
  that!

1*st October*, 1910.

DARTYMOOR.

ZO mark my word these tales be fine
  O' Dartymoor an' tor an' farm,
Gert pool an' hugeous wambling pine
  An' kicklish tangled zunzet warm.

Its wonnerful this bestest clutch
  O' tale o' tilth an' hole an' tarn,
O' leery looking oaf an' such,
  An' furze-gorse catched to hatch mouthed barn.

Way backalong to Bellaford
  Wigged weathers crop the spangled down,
Bell'd hosses jog wi' snort an' gaud
  All truck-a-muck to Totnes town.

The blind tors notch the wilderness
  In purple mist o' snow-cloud foam,
This instant moment (jukes-a-mess!)
  Sucks up the sky to Widdicombe.

The come along o' it be zo—
  Grey gaffers niffed to wedlock gall
An' missuses down daunted go
  Wi' gilt wore off the ginger ball.

Curmudgeons o' but ill botched bone,
  An' turps in barr'ls blazing hell,
An' wench in clouts as baint her own,
  An' crookd ghost hutchd to Crazywell.

All hugger mug the gleaners toil,
  (We'm seed 'em but a bit ago).
Lil childer roam the cowslip'd goyle
  Red pinnered in a handfast row.

Lil treasures o' the shiny eyes
  Zo blue, you hear the harebells ring
To elfin music rare an' wise,
  An' laughter loitering 'long the ling.

Squat toadstones dugged to Lether Tor
  In mizzling mirk o' zunzet red.
Oh, dally buttons— Dartymoor
  For sure be terrible fine spread!

Its wonnerful this clutch o' tricks
  By Mister Villpotts writ zo grim,
Us baint slack twisted daps o'ricks,—
  We'm terrible concerned to him.

Us baint born fools, an', rightful like,
We 'me going to ax to Thacker Spinks
For this fierce book o' crag an' dyke,—
An' us'll tell 'ee what us thinks.

But Mister Villipotts be good,
An' Mister Murray stram-bang grit,—
We'm minded now o' Walna wood
By Dart along to Merripit.

Pied pony pads, wi' lads astride
In corduroy, come by our way,
Hisself has tell't where vixen hide
In Runnage hurst by Babenay.

We baint annointed fools for zo!
We'me Devon maid an' bacheldor—
Vill'd zider pots, swig "Ho, so ho,"
To Villipotts an' Dartymoor!

(From a Review of "Tales of the Tenements" by Mr. Eden Phillpotts.)

The Englishman, 3rd October 1910.

GREEK UNSEENS.*

WHEN I was but a little boy I knew TUPTO TUPTOMENOI,
And took a header, helter skelter, in A. B. G. Δ.
Or else a monumental joy in TO KALON or OI POLLOI—
While stuffing up my mental *bureaus* with gentle paulo-post-futuros.
Then floundered all around at ease in BACCHÆ of Euripides.
(The only 'bacca now I knows is 'bacca from Macropolo's.)
I tackled stout Antiphanes at learned Aunty Fanny's knees,
But, Antigone (that's Aunty Fan) I cottoned up to Lucian.
She taught me how to print in prose, Lucydides and I did "O.'s"
We read Meander, just we two ('twas me and 'er not me and you).
But never bothered about Plato and now alas it is too late—o.
Iambic verse is naught to me (Iambiculiar you see)
And lost illusive "Greek unseens" are much lamented might have beens.
Alas, alas, I've quite forgot the Liddell I mugged up from Scott;
For Greek to me has never caught on, not as it ought GNOTHI SEAUTON.

The Englishman, 10th October 1910.

*** From a Review of "Greek Unseens." By Mr. W. Lobban.**

"ALICIA."*

"Alicia's hobby for some years has been the collection of recipes for cakes and puddings—and a very good hobby too. These are now given to the world with the advice to take care in the actual mixing and cooking. All you then want is a Rippingill stove, and an even temper. When "Alicia" comes in at the door dyspepsia flies out at the window."

THIS column's not too long I think
To praise a book from Thacker Spink
That comes to lift dyspeptic gloom—
A booklet with the *nom-de-plume*
"Alicia."

"Trust not the *bobachee*," it cries,
"But engineer your own mince pies,
For *chota hazris*, *tiffins*, teas
From these well tested recipes."
"Alicia."

Its price a dib, its covers green
With pages sixty-three between,
'Twill sweeten all your afternoons
With maraschinod macaroons.
"Alicia."

"Stir well and add vanilla spice
Then mix with chopped pistachio ice!"
(Such sound remarks are good to see
And just the thing for you and me.)
"Alicia!"

And so on my best bookshelf lies
This tested tale of priceless pies—
They take the cake or nab the bun
(I haven't tasted every one.)
"Alicia!"

The Englishman, 17*th October* 1910.

---

* From a Review of "Our Afternoon Teas." By "Alicia."

BEAUTIFYING THE MAIDAN.

* The *Englishman* and the *Journal* had published a number of letters commenting adversely upon a suggestion made by "Dâk" to erect a new Town Hall, on the model of the Birmingham Hall, on the site of the Outram Statue in Chowringhee, and the Corporation had officially announced that the acquirement of another, and less suitable site would cost Rs. 22,00,000. Calcutta's first "Potted Play" was being extravagantly advertised at the time.

To My Critics.

O, YE, who pot and prick and joke
And peck and prod and patter,
O, callow brood of funny folk—
Whatever is the matter?

The wiles of "local fooldom's" ways
Are odd, though exercising,
They "wiggle wog" like potted plays
With sultry advertising.

"Quot homines sententiæ tot,"
"V. E." and Co. so clever—
Go on—squib, squat and blot a lot
For ever and for ever.

When Lilliput wields tomahawks,
And "Quots" and "Tots" turn talkers,
It's not the least affair of "Dâk's,"
Though fun for tomahawkers.

All "doublegees" and "doublevees,"
And tomahawked "V. E." lings
Like Tweedledums and Tweedledees
Must ventilate their feelings.

It doesn't matter, not a bit,
The quarry who is hunted,
The quarry merely smiles at it—
The tomahawks get blunted.

So tootle tootle to your fill
And puff your little ribs out,
Wind follied horn and pickled quill
And wear your little nibs out.

The prose is read, the ads are blue,
  And "fooldom's" wisdom scrappy—
The *maidan's* green—O, go on do—
  It seems to make you happy.

The Journal, 30th October 1910.

THE DEVIL AND THE DEEP SEA.*

JOHN Greene he was a nice young rogue
  Who fell in love in haste;
And Susan Field was in the vogue,—
  She had a wasp-like waist.

While Susan's ways were all her own,
  As Susan's waist was slim,
He left poor Susan all alone
  Though she went trumps on him.

Through chapters twelve they coo and sigh
  And little comes to pass.
Did she at last a Greene Field die
  Or as a widow (grass)?

The Englishman, 31st October 1910.

FIAT LUX.

"Mr. Payne, the Acting Chairman of the Corporation, in his letter to the Board of Directors after describing the procedure adopted in making the deductions, says: 'I inspected the lighting on a large number of occasions and it was so bad that it would not be an exaggeration to say that considerably more than half the lamps were really defective. On several occasions we were accompanied by your Manager, Mr. Watson.' The latter admitted that the street lighting was bad."—*The Englishman*, yesterday.

MR. Payne, with the manager, went as detective,
  Inspected the system and found it defective.
"More than half of it's wrong"—said the Chairman—"that's plain!"
Mr. Watson observed "I observe it with payne!"
Then the Chairman on bills made some payneful deductions.

*** From a Review of "The Devil and the Deep Sea," by Miss Rhoda Broughton.**

The Gas Co. resented, and now there are ructions.
It's clear that the gas isn't clear—a fiasco;
They've cut down the *tallop* and cut up the Gas Co.
The gas in the main in the main's a thin stuff.
The gas in the Council is more than enough.
The Council-tap's on, overflowing and dreaded.
In the street lamps are off, though a few are light headed—
While the town's in the dark till again reassured
By the Board that no longer by gas 'twill be bored,
Though no one supposes the Board a deceiver.
It's tricks are not due to a gastricky fever.
It loves Mr. Watson, adores Mr. Payne,
They have done what they could, with their might and their
main
To light up the town, and enlighten the folk
With reports and retorts and discussions on coke.
A truce to retorts, the town's cornered, and tightly.
The fiat's "be quiet—case *pendente lite!*"
Fiat Lux, that is all it can hope for or pray,
Though it's still very clear that it's not in luck's way.

The Englishman, 4th November 1910.

---

* BEAUTIFYING THE MAIDAN AGAIN.

NOW "doublegee" and "doublevee"
Don't "medal'" any longer,
"Dak's" two of you—he's "double you" (see ?)
And bound to prove the stronger.

Last week he lent you tomahawks
To wage your little battles,—
That was a mild mistake of "Dak's"
He should have sent two rattles,

For tomahawks an "dawkward" toys
With points and edges stop fun;
If you grow up and are good boys
He'll buy you each a pop-gun.

The Journal, 6th November 1910.

---

* *Vide* note to verses of previous week.

THE JOLLY ROGER.

" Lord Morley has been appointed Lord President of the Council. Lord Crewe is Secretary of State for India."

" Reuter " **yesterday.**

THE Captain goes, recedes from view,
The helm is taken by the Crewe.

This sort of thing, it seems to me,
Is politics' epitome.

From out the fight the Generals drop.
The rank and file are now up top.

The Statesman gone, the wise and great,
The crowd command the strings of State.

While delegates assume the reins,
And parish-pumpers forge the chains.

The " skull and bones " are flying fast,
The " Jolly Roger" 's at the mast.

O, despot John, why did you go
To Runnymede and act like so ?

Come back, come back, my regal boy,
You 're better than the *oi polloi.*

Forgive, royal Sire, baronial slips—
We'll tear that Charter up in bits.

Come back, Oh bless your despot pate,
But hurry up, it's not too late !

The Journal, 6*th November* 1910.

SIGHMOANA AND PASQUINO.

(*A rigidly condensed version.*)

MAIDEN she of Florence City,
Name Sighmoana—rather pretty.
He Pasquino—all her own-a
Spooned about with Miss Sighmoana.
Then, so say the Tuscan letterers,
" Passion's fire " (with all *et ceteras*).

Strolling on the lawn, they two,
Quinny plucked a leaf to chew
(Stupid sort of thing to do)
Smacked his hand across his head
Crumpled up and tumbled dead—
(So the papers went and said).

People cried " it's like her cheek!"
Ran her in before the beak.
So she stood inside a dock
Going on like one o'clock.
" This here leaf's " she said, said she
" 'S what he swallered just like me."
Rubbed her lips as if in fun,
Tumbled dead as he had done.

The Journal, 7th November 1910.

AN " ASIAN MYSTERY."

" Not far from the saluting point at Wednesday's review of troops, there stood, until lately, a clump of some four or five trees. Recently coolies have been busily employed there, and the trees with one exception have been cut down and carted away. . . . If they were removed, as it would appear, merely for the convenience of troops, manœuvring at a single review, the matter can only be characterised as a scandal."—*The Asian.*

O woodman spare that tree
  Nor lop, nor chop one bough,
We've lost the other three
  Or four, so stop it now.

We've lots of things to lop
  And lose without a moan,—
One thinks of quite a crop,—
  But leave the trees alone.

That clump on the *Maidan*
  Pure thing of joy now slain;
Long ministered to man,
  Long glorified the plain.

It whispered hope of God
  Who cares for man and bee
And bird and beast and sod—
  O, *mistree* spare that tree.

The Empire, 21st November 1910.

TWO AT THE TOP.

Scene. Private Smoke-room of Government House, Calcutta.
Time. Monday, 21st November 1910. 11 45 P.M.
Present. Lord Minto and Lord Hardinge.

LORD MINTO. (*As last attendant lets the purdah drop behind him*)
"Alone, my Lord," (*pushing match-box forward*)
"relight, the night is young." "So here's (*standing up*)
THE KING!"

LORD HARDINGE, (*also rising*) "THE KING!"

BOTH TOGETHER. "THE KING!" (*reseat themselves.*)

L. M. "Fine view, out there," (*indicates by a wave of the hand grounds with Maidan beyond.*)

L. H. "So wide, serene, and still."

L. M. "That's India there, wide, silent and superb—
That's India now.—And so you caught the train?"

L. H. "By just a chance,—ha! ha!—it was a shave."

L. M. "A narrow shave, a miss"—

L. H. "Is just as good as—
"Miles—"

L. M. "The "Persia" sung?"

L. H. "A wherry taut."

L. M. "And Clarke?"—

L. H. "Dear Man!"

L. M. "And she?"

L. H. "A charming bride."

L. M. "Hot work at home!"

L. H. "All London's up again—
And Fleet Street's bellowing like a Bashan bull—
On hind legs reared and Stead and Hardie and—"

L. M. "He called on me"— (*shrugs shoulders*).

L. H. "And did he really though?" (*puffs.*)

L. M. "He did—but give me Bepin or Surrendranath—
Re-light (*hands silver-bound box of cigars*). To business
May I offer this? (*hands cutter*) and this? (*hands ash-tray*) and this? (*hands matches again*).
And may I offer tips? I know the ropes."

L. H. "My Lord, your tips are just the things I need" (*bends forward expectantly*).

L. M. (*Leaning back in chair and watching the cheroot smoke curling upwards*) "You know there's been the mischief, Sir, to pay. (*Puffs.*)
You know what India is, or think you do.
I thought I did at first. I'm wiser now—
(*Gravely.*) The strain's tremendous—"

L. H. (*Lowering cheroot*) "Sir, I know that strain,
I know the feel when to the world you show
A still calm face, a front to quell alarm,
But in the silence of a room, (*puffs*)—alone,—(*puffs*)
You clutch the arm-rests of your chair to nerve
Yourself to—"
L. M. "Push beyond you to the dark
The thought of what has been and what may be."
(*Suits words with action.*)
L. H. "Like that, my Lord; Sir Andrew knew that feel."—
L. M. "And Fuller—"
L. H. "Ah:"
L. M. "*And Fuller*. Yes, he did." (*Both pause.*)
L. H. "So Kitchener's been going it, it seems ?"
L. M. "Great K.—St. George's and Sir Archibald !" (*Both chuckle.*)
L. H. "She'll turn up yet."—
L. M. "They say that some-one finds"—
L. H. "Some mischief still for"—
L. M. "Idle hands, ha ! ha !"
L. H. (*Looking at watch*) "It's getting late. Those lights out there—a fire ?"
L. M. "The Docks and Alipore"—
L. H. And Alipore ?
"Where that big trial came off, and Eardley Nort—?
L. M. (*Smiling*) "There's naught on now. It's over, that's all done."
L. H. (*Eagerly*) "And thanks to you, and thanks to you, I say."
L. M. "You're very kind"—
L. H. "You saw the road to take
And stuck to it, my Lord"—
L. M. "You're very kind"—
L. H. "'Twas dogged did it. Grit. Good British grit."
L. M. (*Solemnly*) "Well, well, thank God, we're through, the land's at rest.
(*Cheerfully*) And here you are to grasp the reins and guide
A world that wakes from dreams we may not plumb.
(*Impressively*) Sit tight, my Lord, I need not say,—ride straight.
Sit tight and top the hurdles one by one,—
Teeth set, whip spared, so long as safety lasts
But hap it so that whip be wanted lash—"
L. H. "And lash and lash"—
L. M. "That's it—"
L. H. "When safety's lost."
"There's trouble Lhassa wards ?

L. M. "There is, go slow,
Watch, watch. The yellow race, like all the East,
May best be coaxed, not driven, never set—"
L. H. "Set by the ears, you mean, at Jingo's whim."
L. M. (*Smilingly*) "*You* know your work. There's Persia derelict
To tax your skill and test your tempered tact"—
L. H. "Trust Russia—"
L. M. "Trust the good that lies at heart
Of all men rightly studied, rightly met.
(*Rising*) Good-night, my Lord, you've had a tiring day."
L. H. (*Throwing back his shoulders*) "It seems a year since Howrah came in sight."
L. M. (*Stretching out both arms*) "It seems a thousand years since Curzon went—
(*Placing hand on the other's shoulder*) You won't want
punkahs now, you know, and some
At this third floor don't need mosquito nets.
A *bearer* waits outside at call all night—"
L. H. "Quite so, and thanks, good night!—"
L. M. "Good night! good night!" (*goes out*).
L. H. (*Peeping round corner of purdah*) "I say, hot water in the morning, eh?"
L. M. (*From a yard or two down the landing*) "Yes, yes, of course, at six o'clock, of course—
We call it *gurrum pani* hereabouts.
You'll get as much of it as you may want, and (*slyly*) more.
Its *gurrum, gurrum, gurrum pani* we
Who rule the East must risk and knowing which,—(*smiles*).
L. H. "We learn to dodge it—" (*laughs*).
L. M. "That we've got to learn"—(*laughs too*).
L. H. "And thanks to pluck, and luck to take no scald.
"Good night, my Lord."
L. M. "Good night, again, my Lord!"
(*Both turn in and a lustrum ends.*)

22*nd November* 1910.

[*h*

" UP AGAIN."

" Lord Hardinge's term as Viceroy is evidently going to be exciting. He provided two little sensations on the platform in London, and yesterday morning had an amusing adventure on the *Maidan*. He fell off his horse and the Commander-in-Chief going to his assistance suffered exactly the same fate! The *aides-de-camp* stood by amazed at these goings on among the mighty; but the mighty, none the worse, picked themselves up laughing merrily."—*The Englishman, 26th November* 1910.

MY beautiful, my beautiful that pranceth sleekly there
The Ellenborough Course is hard, and then this isn't fair,—
Fret not to roam the *maidan* now at full Viceregal speed,
I mean to mount on thee again, thou art ' sold ' my waler steed.
I nearly got my pocket picked, I nearly missed my train,
I nearly, very nearly lost my hold upon thy rein,—
Away the dew is on the grass, away before the breeze,—
We'll watch the woodmen where they whack a-chopping down the trees.
We know each other better now, away, away we go:
O'Moore's the most politest of the C.-in.-C.'s I know,
The nimblest officer I've met, away, away, away—
I'm up again, he's up again, agile Sir O'Moore Creagh.

The Journal, 27th November 1910.

THE LYNX.*

LISTEN to me the Demon said,
And rubbed his hyacinthine head,
Of Libyan region lone and lean
And Zäire rushing sub-terene
In slime and essences obscene
With opalescent things between.

The waters of the prism'd stream
In saffron'd dew of wondering dream
To tumult and confusion run
Beneath the red eye of the sun,
When day's monotony is done,
With spikenard melting one by one.

*** From a Review of " Edgar Allan Poe " by Mr. Arthur Ransome.**

Tall trees, primeval, shake and sigh
Where rootless herbs dry rotting lie,
They claw, as hags, the amber air,—
No wind but waileth unaware
Of raven rude to cloak despair,
There is no quiet, no silence there.

And overhead a crescent cloys,
Pale Genii meet in equipoise
The melancholy Magi round
Vague velvet volumes brazen bound.
No silence there, nor yet no sound.
No baying of a bood-fanged hound.

The sayings of the Sybils hold
The thing of lore as flasks of gold—
Of Dodona on trembling knees
And mildewed leaves of whispering trees
That drink great sobs in varying keys,
To silver throated harmonies.

The Catacombs of Ptolemais
Yield shrouded hosts in shadowy guise,
And people, lewd ironical,
The foul Charonian canal,
Where agates analytical,
Point quadrants quaint and bestial.

The Demon ended in grimace,
The tomb'd Lynx looked him in the face.
O, Ulalume! O, lost Lenore!
O, Annabel! I'm very sure
I'd better discontinue, for
The *Englishman* won't stand no more!

The Englishman, 28th November 1910.

"MAX" QUACKS.

"Speaking for myself I should be inclined to say that *Dâk Dicta* will prove to be one of the events of the century. Until I perused this book I was under a misconception as to what poems really were. I am now enlightend and can say with Simeon 'Lord now lettest thou thy servant depart in peace for where ignorance is bliss 'twere folly to be wise'!"—"Max" in *Capital*, 1*st December* 1910.

OLYMPIAN "Max" the matchless sweeps
Calcutta's main to nether deeps—
Perched paramount above the din
To net us little fishes in.

I sent no book : my work's enough
To push itself without his puff,
Nor knelt to " Max " with " if you please
Review this thing in journalese !"

Reviews are just the things to pay ;
They lubricate the wheels to-day ;—
Unasked he's tipped one off his bat
And chanted a *magnificat*.

He's boomed me with a bolt benign,
Out ladled blessings leonine
With caudal wags to point his love,
And roared like any sucking dove.

I've wondered, more than once or twice,
Why he's cut up uncommon nice.
What moved the heart within those ribs
To spend a trinity of dibs ?

" Max " strides the town, pervades the tide
To criticize with proper pride
Our ways, our stage, our church, our mess,
Our Corporation and our press.

He strikes the star-bespangled voids,
He bumps against the asteroids,
Illumes the milky way at night,
And sets good Mr. Apcar right.

A hundred eyed in *Current Chink*,
A hundred armed with printing ink,
He steps around 'mong coals and jutes
A jovial Jupiter in boots.

It seems there was one vacant niche
In that Titanic cranium which
I've filled, and now no room remains
For further wisdom in those brains.

They used to " misconceive " and leak
For years a bit, each wondering week :
Colossal chance ! stupendous " gup !"
I've filled that niche. I've bunged it up.

To think that I have swelled the weight
Of wisdom in that potent pate!—
To think I've added to his store
A thing he didn't know before.

He's perfect now, superb, compact,
I've taught him just the scrap he lacked
And wound him up to seek delights
In scaling proud Parnassus' heights.

No longer poking pens and pins
And tenterhooks in peoples' shins
He'll float aloft on clouds instead
With lots of laurel round his head.

Pegasus, thing of peg and gas
With minor poets oft skids alas,
But "Max's" lyre betwanged will wing
Right bang slap up like anything.

With Orpheus sharing song and shelf
He'll thump the big drum by himself,—
And we shall sigh "for this release
Much thanks!"—and let him go in peace.

2nd December 1910.

"THE LADY FROM GAY PAR-EE."

["It seems hardly credible that anyone should mistake cocoanut husks for tobacco. It appears from a case which came before the courts in Paris that cigarettes made from cocoanut husks had been placed on the market. A female vendor was charged with manufacturing in contravention of the tobacco monopoly, and sentenced to a fine of £100 each on four separate counts. It was at this trial that the extensive character of the cocoanut husk cigarette trade was brought out."—*The Englishman*, *28th November* 1910.]

LIST! a little mistake
Of a maid on the make;
A prodigal girl of Par-ee,
Who, the papers report,
Was presented at Court
And amerced in six hundred rupee.
To *la ville Lumière*
From her *père* and her *mère*
She chirrupped *tra-la la lala;*
Then she worked up the husks
From the pigs with the tusks
Into smokes for the Paris *bazar.*

This trade I regret
In the gay cigarette
Fell flat and a trifle expensive.
A cocoanut jars
Pounded up for cigars,
Be its character merely "extensive."
Back, *la-lala-la*
To papa and mama
Went the lady from Par-ee so *jolie.*
It's the stupidest joke
Turning husks into smoke
Controverting a French monopoly.

Now, scorning cheroots,
She goes banking at Coutts,
And drives each afternoon on the *Bois.*
At *les* "Follies Bergères"
Spurns *le vin* ordinaire
For *Perrier Fils, le bon soir.*
There is milk in a nut
And we know it, but—but
We never know how it gets there.
Still it's nothing to you,
Nor yet to me too,—
It's merely the lady's affair.

So I spread the renown
Of the cocoanut brown,
(But whatever's gone wrong with the type ?)
And I'm glad she was fined
For she's hardly the kind
One would fancy to fill up a pipe.
She failed at a fake
And she made a mistake
And the cocoanut stands on its head
With a "character" big
(Which is nuts for the pig)
Upside down—so *The Englishman* said.

You may rig the *bazar,* if you don't mind a fine,
But don't prig the husks from the poor little swine.

The Asian, 3rd December 1910.

"AN EARLIER BIRMINGHAM."

"And the conveyances and the drivers of Allahabad, the City of God. The *garries*, *ticca garries*, packing cases upon wheels, packing cases that of a certainty held fittings for the Ark of Captain Noah, bought in an earlier Birmingham!"—*The Englishman, 30th November* 1910.

"Tubal-Cain an instructor of every artificer in brass and iron."—*Genesis iv.* 22.

AN earlier Birmingham,—a dream of immemorial past,
The *Englishman* has been and gone and dug it from the vast.
The site of Ararat is found, its whereabouts are clear,
It's somewhere in the Midland Zone in western Warwickshire.

Though boxed up in a packing case where ticca garries creep,
The *Englishman* reveals a sort of pre-historic peep.
It seems that long before the Flood of Japheth, Shem, and Ham,
There was an Ironopolis—an earlier Birmingham.

You've but to rove round Allahabad, the "town of God" to find
You're graced with that impressive gift an antiquarian mind.
You've got to trundle in a cab round Pillar'd Minto Park
To properly appreciate the story of the Ark.

When Zillah, wife to Lamech, kissed her little Tubal-Cain,
She never saw in him a sort of Joseph Chamberlain.
Did Tubal, chief artificer in brass and iron wrought,
Found England's mid-metropolis? Exzillahrating thought!

And have I struck a truth and earned a big historic badge
Like Rev. Mr. Firminger, or Mr. Walter Madge?
Oh, had I Jubal's lyre I'd strum of Brum, and things like that,
Of Tubal-Cain and Chamberlain and Arks and Ararat.

The Indian Planters' Gazette, 3rd December 1910.

ST. SHIRLEY.

According to to-day's *Englishman* Mr. Shirley Tremearne, at the meeting of the Corporation yesterday, said he was willing to pledge himself as a prisoner or hostage for the safety of His Majesty the King-Emperor.

'TIS well to learn of heroes bold
When touring with a man from Cook's
Who shed the glow of ages old
To glorify historic nooks,—
Of Joan of Arc, and William Tell,
Casabianca and Parnell.

If you should go to Rome and glide
With guide by tawny Tiber's hum,
Or linger at the Forum's side,
Or seek the slope Janiculum
    You'll note a slab by tourists thumped
    Denoting where a Roman jumped

Into a gaping hole, dark spread,
Athwart the Forum's ample track,
A big brass helmet on his head,
Astride a noble charger's back;
    He smiled at Fate and leaped in style,
    His steed's eyes bulging out the while.

I've seen the picture of this man;
He filled a gulf by some mishap
That gaped across the paved maidan,
And closed it up—a plucky chap—
    His exit was a trifle crude
    But then he won Rome's gratitude.

A lesson lurks somewhere around
This fine heroic escapade;
If you for Rome go underground
She never lets your memory fade.
    She ne'er forgets the episodes
    Of men used up in mending roads.

And now a new Patrician comes
To claim an Empire City's thanks,
A bearded Nestor snaps his thumbs
At Wyness, Simmons, Roy, and Banks
    "You want a hostage, Sirs!" says he
    Then (with a sob) "I'm here. Take me!"

His folded fists across his chest,
He sank within his *edile* chair,
He was the very very best
Of all the wise Patricians there.
    The well upholstered chair went crack
    With golden adjutants at back.

Then *toga'd* Maddox, tapping teak
That tops the *rostrum*, dabbed his eyes.
Each golden bird with golden beak
Flapped, one by one, towards the skies.
    And Payne and Dutt and all the rest
    Ejaculated "Well I'm blest!"

And Cohen seemed a bit unnerved
And Rae observed "Hurray!" "Grand Slam!!"
"He's capital—by Jove!" observed
The Moulvic Seraj-ul-Islam.
And Shelton muttered "I declare—"!
(I'm wrong, for Shelton wasn't there.)

About his neck they wound a rope,
And bade him sleep on mouldy hay;
Curtailed his soup, and cut his soap,
And took his spectacles away.
And Mookerjee beneath the chair
Wept "So be it,—it's his affair!"

With drooping lid, and flinchless port
He hied him to his pallet straw,
He was the very nicest sort
Of hostage that I ever saw;
So Bertram thinks and Braunfield too
And everybody—me and you.

The golden birds with golden beaks,
Those augurs whom the gods advised,
Will not return for several weeks
(Or so the newspapers surmised)
They've gone to bring (the papers told)
A halo for St. Shirley bold.

9th December, 1910.

CROMWELL AND MILTON.

"He (Mr. Birrell) says there is a print one sees about representing Oliver Cromwell dictating a despatch to John Milton, and that it is all imagination, as there is nothing to prove that Cromwell and Milton were ever in the same room together, or exchanged words with one another. Thus perishes one of my earliest beliefs. I have another larger and finer print. It belonged to my father, and represents Cromwell refusing the Crown in a pillared chamber of Whitehall, and according to the index plate among the spectators is John Milton. A long time ago I sent a description of this print to *Notes and Queries*, when the Birrell-Milton-Cromwell controversy was going on, and succeeded in adding fuel to the anti-Birrell fire. Further favourable comment is needless. "*Obiter Dicta*" is almost the best "*Dicta*" on the market."—From "Dâk" on "Obiter Dicta" in the *Englishman*, *12th December* 1910.

I have a picture ageing brown
Concerning Cromwell and the Crown;
It hung within the house, I know
Where I was born some years ago.

The Crown is looking rather smart,
And Cromwell's hand's on Cromwell's heart,
Says he, "Oh take that thing away
I'm not accepting Crowns to-day!"

Close by with ringlets like a girl's
Sits Milton, lord of quills and curls;
While all around in wigs and pokes
Stand generals and important folks.

And yet, Augustine Birrell, yet
You still assert they never met,
You'd have me both my eyes distrusting—
Augustine, this is too disgusting.

The Welsh attorney's on the bound,
And Redmond flings *shillelahs* round,
Redoubtable Sir David Rees
Is feeling shaky at the knees.

The Lords are looking blankly blue—
Though Balfour says, "I'll pull you through!"
While ladies with precision neat
Are butchering panes in Downing Street.

In spite of this, in spite of all
My picture's there upon the wall,—
Augustine Birrell, Ireland's Chief,
You've tried to shake my first belief!

Obiter Dicta—be it known,—
I've got *Dâk Dicta* of my own!
I really hope you don't get in.
I hope the other man will win.

12th December, 1910.

THE CAMEL, OR A FRIEND IN EED.

"Parading the streets in the disturbed quarter of Calcutta on Saturday in rear of the 16th Cavalry was a magnificent Camel."—*The Englishman, 12th December* 1910.

TO pray is better than to sleep.
The glowing camp fire reds the dawn—
Eed-uz-zoha, the people keep
The *Eed* on this *muezzin'd* morn.
Bright Cavalry *en bivouac*.
A Camel with a twisted back.

The East is East. The West is West:
The guarded mosque's *Korbani* feast:
Whatever is is best, is best:
The West is West. The East is East.
    The English mounted squadrons riding near.
    A splendid Camel in the rear.

The houses barred, the drums proclaim
The cow will die; the Brahmins moan
The vexed gods, swinging camphor flame
Through chill fog to the shrill shawms blown.
    The Cavalry and Camel pace
    The causeway in this year of Grace.

The worshippers on matted knee
Swarm dense, gold, green and white and red,
And hues of velvet sunset sea
Bright blended in chaotic spread.
    True prayer flies swift to Allah's gate.—
    The Cavalry and Camel wait.

The gaunt Kabuli bending shrugs
With blood-daubed beard and prayer, confessed
A craving penitent, but tugs
At looted jewel in beaten breast.
    The Camel and the Light Horse rein
    To cavalcade a shuttered lane.

Along the lane the lancers glide,
The packed Marwaris hold to home,
The stuffed *morgue* flings red barrier wide
For droning bearers where they come.
    The sabred riders shine in state.
    The Camel steps with sneer sedate.

The *Moulvies* pray for Hardinge, Lord,
For Baker *Sahib* this Bakr-Eed,
For Halliday whose guardian ward
The Faithful holds from harm at need.
    The Amratollah mosque shews fine
    With horse and Camel line on line.

We linger in this land of pain,
We, England's sons, who may not tell
The secret of her cold disdain,
The cruel conundrum of her spell.
    The Bakr-Eed is dead and done.
    The Cavalry and Camel gone.

The secret lives, it cannot die;
The East is East. The Minaret
Mocks white the calm cerulean sky
Star-pointed, while the gods forget.
    Our horsemen sweep the Orient, blind.
    The Camel clatters on behind.

To read the riddle and to learn
The lore of purple Orient pearled,
To lift the veil, the creeds discern—
The crowding creeds of half the world—
    Ask not the riders reining gay.
    The Camel knows, but may not say.

Walk careless of masqued politics,
Nor heed religion worn without,
Their way yields halfpence less than kicks,
There're far too many sorts about.
    The Cavalry cremate no *joss-stick*.
    The Camel's a confirmed agnostic.

Gird, gird for war a Peace to keep—
A maxim true.—Drub, drub the drum!
Both East and West guard clear from sleep
The *Odium Theologicum*.
    The Cavalry patrol from view.
    The Camel hath a Maxim too.

Calcutta, 12*th December*, 1910.

---

*ONE LITTLE NOON.

FULL thrice a hundred moons refulgent-bright
    Have shook pale tresses to a star-stabbed night
Since first I passed the Orient's lintelled door
To tread the gemmed mosaics of her floor.

The East then lay inscrutable, confessed
Unknowable, unknown of wandering West.
I go :—the East a world of loved regret
Unknown, unknowable, enigma'd yet.

---

* Written within a few hours of retirement to England.

I go, the graspless East still luring lies
A golden glory webbed in wonder skies,—
And thank the gods for grant of the high boon
To touch her raiment's hem one little noon.

Calcutta, 19*th December* 1910.

PART II.

PHILATELIC.

I have met with curious philatelic survival, an unsullied delightful whiff from a dead age, a philatelic pre-historic peep not often to be enjoyed now, to wit a "Lallier" album of the early sixties with a small collection of the stamps of those days, cut to shape where considered necessary, pasted well down and obviously thumped upon.

The charm of the old "Lallier" has never, in spite of its wicked little ways, been quite equalled by that of its scientific well set up successors, of ordered neatness and exasperatingly machine-made regularity. No Englishman could have perpetrated such a joyfully irresponsible arrangement between covers. Its uncouthness is superb; the rough paper, the irregular spacings, the cramped up catalogue with quaint lettering, the uncalled for "coats-of-arms." And yet such is the spell woven by the individuality of the work that you can't help liking it. The world went very well then with "timbro-maniacs" as we were called; and the "album-timbres-poste par Justin Lallier" ran to thirteen editions between 1863 and 1876, the first French and English editions having both appeared in Paris in 1862. For Justin had ways of his own. He not only turned out a capital album bearing in mind the limited range of philatelic knowledge possible to him, but he initialled the copies sold with his own sign-manual in a scrawly French way and refused to correct obvious errors in following editions in spite of British criticism—the dear good obstinate man.

What a world of memories the little drab oblong volume revives; turn the time-tinted pages very very tenderly and thank God the white ants have never got to them.

It is an autumn day in 1865. My brother and I are "doing stamps." I am but a little fellow, proud of my first knickerbockers, and he is thrice my age, but I know his "Lallier" page for page and stamp for stamp as well as he does and it is a brave book indeed. He gives me a few stamps, Hongkongs, we have relatives in China and so Hongkongs to us are "drugs on the market," and I, with all the pride that only a collecting soul can feel, fix them up on a sheet of white paper ruled just as the page of the Lallier is ruled, placing them in the correct order and proper positions, and after thumping upon them with the orthodox thumps of the genuine collector, it all seems too good to be true and looks just like the real thing, though the effect is perhaps marred by the addition of a big blue British fiscal from off a receipted butcher's bill.

That morning is our last together. A few days pass, it may be a week, and there is a great stillness in the house for the eldest son is dead.

Thus my stamp collection began, and it still includes one at least of those identical Hongkongs. It is a far cry back to November, 1865, but I have been true to my stamps as Hongkong has been true to hers and she has never changed.

My brother, Charles Winter Corfield, must have been among the earliest of English stamp collectors; he left behind him a choice collection which a few years after his death was incorporated with mine.

His stamps were all picked specimens and arranged with the approval of the great E. L. Pemberton himself. A black Nicaragua from among them is still one of my most cherished sentimental delights.

It is several years later. The "Lallier" is my very own now. We are at a Welsh watering place. It is a summer afternoon, and the newsboys come running from the railway station with the Birmingham newspapers. My father buys one hurriedly, a little rush of people form round, he speaks aloud and there is a catch in his voice as he reads—"WAR DECLARED, THE EMPEROR HIMSELF TAKES THE FIELD." I can see the faces of the people now, and hear the shouts of the newsboys selling their tidings along what was called "the Marine Parade"—and then some-one mentions Eugénie.

I run back, I take out my "Lallier," the sun has gone down. Yes, here is France and here he is, green and orange and blue and carmine—quite a lot of him, and this is the Emperor. The sea across the parade is swirling strong and black, there are white tufts of foam, and above the sky-line a narrow strip of opal and amethyst leads up to a great dull sullen mass of cloud. The cloud grows bigger and bigger, and its rugged upper edge jags off into suggestions of banner and bayonet as of a host passing. There is lightning too and thunder and here is my "Lallier," and this is the Emperor, and I conjecture (wrongly as it happens) that France is somewhere over there just where the lightning is forking now. And Eugénie ? I have a picture of her at home—she is playing croquet in a scarlet and gold zouave jacket, a shining chignon, and an entrancing crinoline, while the little Prince Imperial is curvetting in the background on a tricycle. It is wrong I know, for she is a papist and worships graven images which Martin Luther who wrote "Tracts for the Times" and most of the 39 articles objected to, but away down at the bottom of my heart I have Oh such a wish that the pretty lady will somehow or other come up top out of the business just beginning.

I still have my Emperor, more than ever of him—green and blue, orange and carmine, and I saw a picture of Eugénie the other day at the Club, she wasn't playing croquet, she was seated in a motor car and talking to some one who goes about in air-ships, and I'm afraid I still feel sorry that things didn't turn out differently.

The date of the beginning of matters philatelic to me having been fixed in my memory by a tragic event I may fairly claim now to be one of the oldest continuous collectors. I have never ceased collecting and never remember selling or exchanging a stamp out of my collection, though, of course, I have removed many in order to replace them by better copies.

Stamp collecting was really collecting in the old days. The power of the purse was less a factor in getting stamps together than the individual effort, we tracked stamps to their lairs then and knew the full charm of the stern relentless chase.

A windfall came to me in 1877, Stafford Smith & Co.'s *Philatelic Quarterly* awarded me their first prize for an essay on the "Benefits arising from Stamp Collecting." According to the *Quarterly's* report my paper opened with the pertinent enquiry "what on earth is the good of gathering together numberless coloured pieces of paper, generally not a square inch in size, with a sort of fringe round the edge and a kind of sticky substance round the back ?" I answered my own question under thirteen heads, and won in a canter a guinea's worth of stamps selected from the firm's approval sheets. I chose Heligolands—I have them yet—they are all reprints. A few months later I tried again in a competition with "A Poem on Stamp Collecting" as its subject. My verses appear elsewhere in this work in a more up-to-date version entitled a 'Philatelic Rhapsody.' *The P. 2* after quoting from them handsomely said my "poem would have been the best were there not two better."

Birmingham, my old home, has always been a leading philatelic centre, and its Philatelic Society, of which I am proud to have been a non-working member for many years, is one of the most progressive in the world. The great pioneers of Philately are associated with the city—Sir Rowland Hill, E. L. Pemberton, E. Shorthouse, C. J. Phillips, W. T. Wilson, and Sir William Beilby Avery. Sir William died in 1909, and his collection was sold for £24,500, at present the record price for a sale at auction of any collection. I well remember its start. His aunt, a Miss Maria Beilby, presented him and my brother, already referred to, with "Lallier" albums, so that I have reason to suppose that both his and my own collections sprang from the same kindly thought of one and the same friend of our families. The two collections in their earliest days were subjects of a pair of boyish rivalries. I wish I could get £24,500 for mine. From articles in the *Philatelic Record* and the *Philatelic Journal of Great Britain* in 1902 and 1903 I find I left Birmingham for London in 1882 and went to Calcutta in 1886 and after going there again in 1893 became an early member of the Philatelic Society of Bengal, which in 1897 was merged in the Philatelic Society of India. I was Treasurer of the Philatelic Society of India during 1897-1898 until Sir David Masson relieved me, and Secretary from 1899 to 1909, and am now a Vice-President. I was Secretary of the Kasauli Stamp Exchange Club (perhaps the most uniformly successful of all the Indian Clubs) from September 1895 to September 1897 and relinquished it to take over for a year or two from the late Major Du Moulin the Secretaryship of the Dum-Dum Club. Among my recollections are the four Exhibitions in Calcutta, 1896, 1897, 1898, and 1908, at all of which I exhibited, and visits paid in 1890 and 1899 to those at London and Manchester. At the conversazione held in the City Art Gallery on the latter occasion I was even immortalized in song by Mr. Harrison Hill—

> **" Stanley Gibbons who's perhaps the largest dealer in the world "**
> **" And Corfield, he's from India where the British flag's unfurled."**

In 1907 I was Secretary of the Minto Fête Philatelic Exhibition in Calcutta, the record of which is a unique one. Hurriedly arranged in order to add to the attractions of Her Excellency Lady Minto's eminently successful philanthropic fête, the stamps sent in for exhibition were none the less so numerous and valuable that the Committee dare not entrust them to the tent accommodation provided for them on the *maidan*, and the exhibition was abandoned. Among the stamps I reluctantly returned to their owners unexhibited was a magnificent selection from H. R. H. the Prince of Wales's private collection.

At my suggestion a special exhibition "stamp" was prepared by the Survey of India Department, its design being adapted from the Edwardian stamps of Canada. This label is illustrated in *Gibbons' Stamp Weekly* for 27th August 1910. Its principal feature is a portrait of Her Excellency Lady Minto.

Another memory is that of a dinner given by Mr. C. J. Phillips at the Hotel Cecil in London on 27th June, 1905, at which Mr. L. L. R. Hausburg, Mr. J. N. Luff and I were the guests of the evening, and at which were also present Major Evans, Lieut. Napier, and Messrs. H. J. Duveen, E. D. Bacon, M. P. Castle, C. J. Daun, H. R. Oldfield, R. B. Yardley, J. A. Tilleard, the late E. J. Nankivell, E. Stanley Gibbons and others. The *London Philatelist* remarks that "the chief of that colossal establishment surpassed himself in providing a banquet that left absolutely nothing to be desired by the most fastidious gourmet." The evening was a very enjoyable one and afforded the host an opportunity for a display of the generous hospitality so widely associated with his name.

As the result of my collaboration with the late Mr. C. S. F. Crofton, I. C. S., the "P. S. of I's" Handbook on "The Adhesive Fiscal and Telegraph Stamps of British India" was published in 1905. It is an elaborate work and evidences the remarkable philatelic insight of the late Collector of Nasik, one of the keenest and most lamented philatelists of his day. I have been a Vice-President of the London Fiscal Philatelic Society since 1904.

The *Philatelic World*, the official organ of the Philatelic Society of Bengal, started in 1894, and I edited it throughout nearly the whole of its course until March, 1897, when it ceased on the appearance of the *Philatelic Journal of India*. The *World* went all over the world and was thought well of by collectors everywhere. The Hon. Mr. C. L. Larmour's name was associated with mine in the editorship, but the character of our editorial partnership may be gathered best by his own words in the *World* (after pressure of other work had compelled my retirement not long before the end came)—"I did really edit this paper once—that was before my good friend Wilmot Corfield joined me in my duties. But that is incorrect, I should say before he allowed his name to be joined with mine, for since that, to me, happy event, he has done all the work and I have done all the smiling. And now he is going to do the smiling, not that he has much time for smiling, for if he had he would not leave me to mourn and moan. Come back some day, good friend, when time will allow you and resume your post as co-editor. The readers of the *P. W.* will be glad and so shall I, I assure you."

In conjunction with Mr. C. F. Larmour, I edited the *Philatelic Journal of India*, the official organ of the Philatelic Society of India, during the greater part of 1898 after which I handed over its charge to Mr. C. Stewart Wilson. I have since, however, been repeatedly associated with its production as a sort of handy man on the spot at times of emergency when the philatelic Olympians into whose hands it has since passed have stood in need of editorial aid. May Mr. E. W. Wetherell, at present the able director of its fortunes, live long and sway the blue pencil for ever.

And yet another philatelic memory lies in the bringing together and arrangement of the stamps of India for the Victoria Memorial Hall, Calcutta. The work was officially entrusted to me, at the time of the visit of H. R. H. the Prince of Wales to Calcutta, and an excellent *nucleus* collection of the stamps of all classes, postal, telegraphic and fiscal of the Imperial issues and those of the Indian Native States has been formed. I had the honour of meeting the Prince personally at the time on the subject of the collection and the Government placed its stores of both obsolete and current stamps at my disposal and collectors also made donations of stamps. At present the collection (the national collection of India) is at a stand-still in common with the erection of the Hall itself. About 50 lakhs of rupees were subscribed under Lord Curzon's auspices for the Hall (and its contents) which will some day be the grandest Indian building of modern times. I am convinced that of the treasures to be enshrined in the Hall,—Statues, Portraits, Pictures, Coins, Arms, Treaties, Banners, Manuscripts, &c.—the Stamps will hereafter be not the least popular, and I am proud of having been the suggester of the collection and the medium for the making of it.

The *Monthly Journal* made way for *Gibsons' Stamp Weekly* in 1908, and its disappearance occasioned my verses printed later on. The *Weekly*, however, is now announced to give place to a restored *Monthly* in 1911, but the following letter from Major Evans, the *doyen* of philatelic Editors, speaks for itself.

LAYTON AVENUE, SYDENHAM,

July 2, 1908.

Dear Mr. Corfield,—I am writing to thank you for your kind and too flattering verses, and at the same time to apologise for and explain their being placed in the position in which you will find them in the last (the very last) number of the *Monthly Journal.* Your M.S. seems to have reached London a little late to have been sent straight to the printers without my hearing anything about it, so that the first time I saw it was in the form of a proof of the cover of the *M. J.*, the day after I had returned the final proof of the inside to the printers. I wrote at once to tell them what arrangements could be made for inserting it in the middle of the number, but unfortunately it was too late as they had begun to print.

I feel as if your friendly compliment, which I most fully appreciate, had been very ungratefully received and that a full explanation of how it happened is due to you. I have told Messrs. Stanley Gibbons that they must give instructions for that cover to be bound in with the volume.

With renewed thanks and kindest regards,

I remain, yours truly,

EDW. B. EVANS.

I have been a member of the Royal Philatelic Society, London, since 1899, and was elected a "Fellow" in 1907.

Calcutta formerly, as recently as even twenty years ago, must have been a veritable "Tom Tiddler's Ground" for the stamp collector. The stories of finds in *godowns* and other holes and corners of the earth are many and often true, but unfortunately, however, I missed the main flood myself. One day in the mid-nineties an excited clergyman (now an Archdeacon), of pronounced philatelic tendencies, and a bright and shining light of our humanising pursuit burst in upon me at the office with a supply of charred envelopes still hot from the flames, coated with early Australians whole and in fragments of the choicest brand. A firm near his church were it seems having a sort of spring cleaning up of ancient records coming down from the forties, and *durwans* were indulging in the luxury of burning fuel worth a fortune when my friend interrupted a parochial morning visitation on a piece of charred paper carrying a brilliant "Sydney View" fluttering into his astonished gaze. The funniest part of the episode consisted in the fact that the late Mr. J. O'B. Saunders of the *Englishman*, a well remembered philatelic specialist, sitting in his *sanctum* during the prolonged conflagration had repeatedly consigned his neighbour's *durwans* to an unpleasant fate owing to the annoyance caused by the smoke of the fire beneath his windows interfering with the even flow of an exceptionally choice assortment of editorial leaders in the making.

Another funny episode I remember occurred in May 1908. I was so long the Secretary of the big Indian Society that experience made me very cautious in the matter of the admission of applicants to membership. People wrote from all parts of India, Ceylon and the gorgeous East, thinking they could join by merely saying they wished to do so. One day I received a letter from Henry McCallum at an apparently private address in Ceylon, intimating his intention to become no less than a Life Member. I wrote back to "H. McCallum, Esq.," very politely and in corrrect secretarial terms asking for the names of his proposer and seconder and referring him to Rule Dash, section Dot, and he replied somewhat stiffly "I conceive that my position as Governor of the Colony is a sufficient guarantee of my respectability." Sir Henry was at once enrolled and I broke the rules on the only occasion in my life during a long and exacting period of office.

A PHILATELIC RHAPSODY.

HO! bid the sounding *tom-tom* bang in Philatelic praise
For Waterlow and De La Rue, in stamp-collecting days!
Sing hey! the metre-gauge, and join in jubilation jig
Philately is on the boom and looms uncommon big!
The Stamp is mightier than the sword (so clip your hinges out).
The Album rocks the world to-day (toss tweezers all about)
On Stanley Gibbons turn your talk, on plates and strips and sets,
And gaily gloat o'er catalogues, and revel in *roulettes*—
Salaam, salaam, the Postage stamp, that magic little label
Whose fame has far outstripped the fame of prehistoric fable;
We're now aware e'en Lemprière ne'er wrote of one so clever,
And still the Stamp is on the ramp for ever and for ever!
We read that Hermes oft was wont (what times the gods were larky)
To saunter round with little *chits* in drab *dak-wallah's kharki*—
That he it was in days gone by who oft was seen to go
And rat-tat-tatter at the doors of Jupiter & Co.
But though his helm was winged, and though he'd wings upon his heel,
'Tis doubtful if he ever showed the courage or the zeal
To face the frosts of Newfoundland, or risk the sorry scrape,
Of dining with the Dutchman whose address is "off the Cape."
Still though the Cape of Storms ne'er woke at passing Hermes' knock,
And though Brazil ne'er knew his call, nor Gib's colossal Rock—
The Cape of Storms, Brazil, the Rock, our modern Mercury know,
For where so e'er man plants his foot there sprouts a G. P. O.
And Jove would soon have sacked the chap who'd donned his postman's livery,
Had Jove but hit on Hill's smart dodge—the Penny Post Delivery.
They talk to us of Icarus—fit theme for scoffer's mirth—
They tell us Atlas' shoulders bore the frame-work of the Earth—
What if they did? Why Love it is that makes the world go round,
So were it not for Love all else would soon come to the ground,
And where would Love be but for Stamps? (come aid me oh, my muse!)
How would the craft of Hymen pay without our *billets doux?*
We read of flying carpets whose motion ne'er fatigues:
Of boots that think just nothing of a stride of seven leagues:

Of winged horses flaming like lightning thwart the sky:
(Of course they could if they had wings, on pinions pigs might fly!)
From these we may some moral point—they may adorn a tale,
But can they hold a candle to our London-Howrah Mail?
The crimson sunset never falls upon our Empire wide,
Rich realms that own old England's rule are swelled by every tide,
To every race the Postage-stamps in gay battalions wend,
On every shore the Stamp is hailed man's "little coloured friend."
The Postal legions wake the world from wondering Pole to Pole,
By Bengal's palm-fringed jungle bunds; where Afric's torrents roll;
In Malta's caverned surf-beat isle; where waves Canadian pine:
On Austral sand encumbered strand; where flows the Cyprian wine;
We own its sway, we bid it speed, at home, at sea, in camp,
That index to our Empire's might, the plucky Postage-stamp;
And though man missed the mystic stone to turn to gold his dross,
Though Alchemy has played him false through years of strain and loss,
He still may dip him deep and wash in bright Pactolian rill,
His talisman the Postage-stamp of good Sir Rowland Hill!

Philatelic World, March 1895.

THE WALRUS AND PHILATELIST.

(*From "Malice through the Pocket-glass."*)

"The * * Rock Ahead * * really looms ominously in the offing and * * threatens to have a disastrous effect upon Philately even if it should not go so far as to make it a total wreck. I allude to the issue of speculative stamps."—Mr. M. P. Castle, in the *London Philatelist, March* 1895.

THE Walrus and Philatelist
Were strolling down the Strand;
They wept like anything to see
A "Rock" there, close at hand:
"If this were only cleared away"
They said, "it would be grand."

"If Mr. C. of the *L. P.*"
"Wrote on for half a year"
"Do you suppose" the Walrus said
"That he could get things clear?"
"I doubt it, Sir!" the other said,
"He couldn't, never fear!"

The Walrus and Philatelist
  Walked on and little said;
But still they gazed upon that "Rock"
  Conveniently ahead;
And all the little Seebecks stood
  And waited there in dread.

Fine French colonials chortled round
  With many a big Obock,
And thick and fast they came at last
  To join the stuff in stock,
All gummed and gay in brave array
  And scrambling to the "Rock."

"It is a shame," the Walrus said,
  "To play this gumbug trick!"
"The joke has gone a bit too far
  It makes a fellow sick—"
"It seems to me his friend remarked
  The Rock's a trifle thick!"

"It's very wrong that dealer-men
  "Won't take our kind advice!"
"It's very queer that dealer-men
  "Have tastes so far from nice!"
"Perhaps it is," the Seebecks said
  "The dealer-men want *pice!!*"

"The time has come," the Walrus said,
  "That retribution brings—"
"The time to jump on Jubilees"—
  "And all these Seebeck things,"
"To write Celestial Locals 'off'"
  "And hint that 'Rocks' need wings."

"But wait a bit," the Seebecks cried,
  "Before you make your sweep,"
"The most of us are unsurcharged"
  And all of us are cheap!!"
"Be off!" shrieked the Philatelist
  And recommenced to weep.

"I weep for you my little friends,
  I deeply sympathise!"
"With sneers and jeers he sorted out
  Obocks of largest size,—"
Holding his patent pocket-glass
  Before his winking eyes.

"Down with the Rock!" the Walrus cried,
"And now we're on the spot"
"Let's pop inside this shop just here"
"And snarl at what they've got!"

Anon they both came smiling out—
They'd been and bought the lot.

Philatelic World, May 1895.

AH SID.

(*The Artful Chinee.*)

YELLOW Ah Sid
A Celestial kid,
With ways that were pensive and vain,
And a freedom from guile
Saw his way for a while
To a means of enhancing his gain:
'Twas an excellent plan
This lemon-faced man
Evolved for enticing the *pice*,
"Um, Cheena-man fly!"
Cried he winking his eye
"Me makee stamp, sell um big plice!"
"Hankow, Chefoo, Chunkiang
Chungking, Wuhuee, Ichang!"
Sang clever Ah Sid,
That yellow skinned kid
And went for Philately—bang!

He made a smart lot
Of designs on the spot,
Of dragons a wriggle, did he,
And threw in all he knew
Of *pagodas* askew,
Did this heathen artistic Chinee.
Small birds with long tails,
And *junks* with trim sails
He planned with alacrity bland,
And cried "me um mash!"
As he raked in the cash
"Me lichee, me glow welly gland!"

" Tientsin, Shanghai, Kewkiang,
Foo Choo, Lia Chih Kwa, Pa Kuang !"
Sang cunning Ah Sid
As he drew them, he did
And up into affluence sprang.

So knowing Ah Sid
The Celestial kid,
Beams child-like and bland all the day,
For his pencil is quaint,
And he dabs on the paint
In a taking Celestial way ;
With tricks that are dark
He'll attach a post-mark
Or surcharge without blushing a jot ;
And he'll chuckle " Ho ho,"
" Me um one two thing know"
" Um, Phlatlee, um pay me, um lot !"
" Wuhu, Hongkong, Candarin,"
" Wufu, Chow Chow, Mandarin,"
Sang busy Ah Sid
That comical kid,
" All samee, me welly much glin !"

Philatelic World, June 1895.

THE CURSE.

The " New Crusade," as it was termed, against unnecessary issues was waged with but little success, and they emerged from the maledictions of a full Vehm Gericht of the S. S. S. S. (the Society for the Suppression of Speculative Stamps), very little the worse for the ordeal. The fact was deplored by all and Major Evans' condemnation in the *Monthly Journal* of the U. S. A. Columbus Jubilees themselves called forth the following :

THE Editor rose from the Editor's nook,
And called for his scissors, his brand and his book ;
In holy anger and pious fret
He solemnly snipped out that rascally set :
Then cursed in " Imperial " accents of dread
Green, purple and brown ; blue, chocolate and red.
He cursed those who keep them, that every night
They should dream of the Seebeck and wake in a fright.
Never was heard such a terrible curse,
But what gave rise to but little surprise
None of them seemed a penny the worse.

Philatelic World, June 1895.

THE APOTHEOSIS OF THE GUMBUG.

A Tale of Ten Years hence.

(*A long way after Kipling.*)

"Imprimis" 'twas a joke. Thereafter came
A dealer firm to boom him, and he boomed;
Then having lost his natural reserve
"Went Seebeck"—joined the postals of the world,
Turned three parts perforate and one imperf
And lived enshined in countless catalogues
Who gave him shelter for a year or twain
And boasted that a *pukka* full blood "stamp"
Had come among them. Thus he spent his time
Deeply beloved of all collector folk
(Who never asked his nature) much surcharged
Unclean, abominable, reprobate,
Pretending that he was a postage stamp.

You know they d—d the Gumbug with a d—,
And every good collector purged his book,
And all the bad material at hand
Was used to fill exchange sheets—which meant *pice*
And therefore profit. Then the Gumbug burst,
And several hundred thousand gross of him
Went down into perdition's valley, "flop,"
And broke a lot of little dealer-men,
And filled a *lakh* or so of magazines
With periodic twaddle. So he passed,
Slain by the clamour of the four S'd league
To philatelic limbo; and we said
We never liked him and it served him right
And moralised about him for a bit
And then forgot him, which was natural.

But with the changing of the century men
Bending o'er ponderous Philatelic hordes
Relate a legend of a big new "find"—
Counting the while each great collection o'er
(In but some five and twenty albums this)
In this wise:—For a space before the find
Man read him in his monthly loved *L. P.*
Or *M. J.* (which you will, it matters not)—
Both Nestors of the Philatelic press,—wherein 'twas writ
In several numbers of a precious thing

Of Philatelic lustre that had been
And gone and got itself evolved wherefrom
Why goodness only knew. And then
A flow of dealers' appro-sheets that bore
Mounted upon their face a curious stamp
That flourishing in mystic power came by
Breathing ambrosia to collector folk—
And simply went for those collector folk—
With zeal beyond the power of pen to put,
On sheets beyond the count of mortal mind,
And smote them with resistless force and drove
Them clamorous ever clamouring for more,
And loomed the biggest boom that ever was,—
And generally cleared men of their tin.
While every journal wrote the wonder up,
And every album bore its counterfeit.
Thus came the wonder to collector folk
Breathing ambrosia, flourishing amain,
It cut out Connell, out V. R'd. V. R.
And cast the best Mauritius in the shade.
And mounted on each wonder-album's page,
And catalogued in countless catalogues,
And gloated o'er by striving folk who watch
Ever alert to own its wondrous charm
It knows itself as well beloved of Heaven.

This is the story of the Gumbug told
With circumstance and some embroidery.

So he the much surcharged, objectionable,
Unclean, abominable, reprobate
Is now a Philatelic deity
To each collector-man of self-respect—
And may in time become a postal myth.

Philatelic World, *June* 1895.

MISBELIEFS.

It will be remembered that "Aliph Cheem" in the "Lays of Ind hints of ohn Bull's misbeliefs concerning India.

> "*That missionary hardships would move you to pity.*"
> "*That tigers are common and ayahs are pretty.*"
> "*And that sweet English girls by the P. and O. carried*"
> "*By hundreds are no sooner landed than married.*"

To which are now added.

THAT elephants prance in the streets of Calcutta
Where leopards and cobras stroll wild in the gutter.
That a *baboo's* a cane and a *moonshee* a rajah,
And a *begum* a *rajah* a little bit larger.

That a *coolie's* a drink and a *gharry* a *hackery*,
That Macaulay was born there (or p'r'aps it was Thackeray);
That all married ladies are flirty though moral;
That breezes are spicy and sea-shores are coral;
That missionaries preach every-day at a palm's base;
That the face of a *nautch-girl* allures with its charm's grace;
That "small service" sets cost at most two rupees;
And "Shere Ali Cabuls" grow in crops upon trees;
And that "half-anna reds" still frank current dispatches
And for five or six *pice* may be raked in in batches.
That furloughs are frequent and salaries grand,—
And the Indian Congress a power in the land.
That *jao*, *chup*, and *tanno* and one or two more
Make the language and each town's a *bad* or a *pore;*
That a *poojah's* a fruit, and that every-thing's *gurrum*,
That Doorga was mated to Mister Mohurrum;—
And that all through the place the great Ganges goes rippling
With the Taj, Alice Gomez, the Kutub, and Kipling.

Philatelic World, September 1895.

SHYLOCK UP TO DATE.

(A FRAGMENT.)

The Customs duty levied on Indian imports presses very hardly on collectors as it insists upon a tariff upon all stamps whether on approval or not coming into the country. The associated collectors of India have again and again approached Government in view to the removal of the Import, but always unsuccessfully.

CHARACTERS :—"*Duke*" *Public Opinion*. "*Antonio*," *Stamp-collector*. "*Shylock*," *Government*.

DUKE : What, is Antonio here ?

ANT. : Ready so please your grace.

DUKE : I am sorry for thee ; for thou hast to tackle
A stony adversary, incapable of yielding,
Void and empty of any grain of pity.

ANT. : I have heard your grace hath ta'en great pains to qualify
His rigorous course ; but since he stands obdurate
And that no lawful means can carry me
Out of his minion's reach, I do oppose
My treasures to his tariff and am armed
To suffer with a quietness of spirit
Th' official tyranny and greed of his.

DUKE (to Shylock) : Shylock the world thinks and I think so too
That thou'lt but learn the spirit of the tariff
To the last clause of th' act ; and then 'tis thought
Thou'lt shew thy mercy and good sense more strange
Than is thy strange apparent selfishness,
And, where thou now exact'st the penalty
(Some five per cent. of good Antonio's cash)
Thou wilt be blind to that the tariff saith
And touch'd with human friendliness wilt wink
Thy dexter optic upon principle.
Glancing the other eye upon his worries,
That have of late so huddled on his back
(Enough to press a royal collector down)
And pluck commiseration of his state
From faking forgers with rough hearts of flint,
From gumbug folk, and seebecks never trained
To tender thought for fair Philately.
We wish a gentle answer don't you know.

SHY. : I have possessed your Grace of what I purpose,
And by our busy Clive Street have I sworn
To have the pue and forfeit of the Act.
If you deny me let my minions light
Upon your baggage and your weekly mails.
You ask me why I rather choose to place
A toll on carrying stamps than to receive
Your thanks to pass them. I'll not answer that
But say it is my orders. Are you answered ?

ANT. : 'Tis a hard answer thou unfeeling man
To curb the current of Philately.

SHY. : I am not bound to please thee with my answer.
I serve the Act. I will not hear thee speak :
I serve the Act, so therefore speak no more.

I am not made of soft and pliant stuff
To shake the head, relent, and sigh and yield
To all your intercessions. Press me not,—
I'll kill the craze—but then I serve the Act!

Philatelic World, November 1895.

LOOKING FORWARD.

(AND BACK ON "J.K.S.")

Oh, for the good time coming:—

WHEN the world shall be delivered from commemorative trash
With the Sydney O. S. shivered and the reprint gone to smash;
When our dripping pens flow freely with each faking forger's gore
When the Seebecks cease from troubling and the gumbugs glare no more.

Philatelic World, November 1895

A RAIL MISTAKE.

THE "A. J. of P."
Says it cannot agree
With the many S'd mentors of Philatelee,
And is forced to confess
That the S. S. S. S.
Missed the points when it shunted that Transvaal Express

Philatelic World, December 1895.

IN MEMORIAM.

ROWLAND HILL.

(Born 3rd December, 1795. Died 27th August, 1879.)

TEN times ten years—ten strenuous years have sped
Since that great heart first throbbed with opening life,
And long mid England's kingliest, saintliest dead,
Has he, strong son of England—slept from strife.—
But still his name shines clear to us and still
We turn in kindly thought to Rowland Hill.

The soldier shares our homage, but his course
Is dark with war's red devastating breath,
And strewn with wreck of home and dying horse
And all the stern grim panoply of death ;—
Fell famine grins on blood with horrid teeth,
And fury weaves the warrior's laurel-wreath.

But "peace hath victories" more lasting far
Than those on battle-scroll emblazoned bright,
Well won by workers mid the strain and jar
Of bloodless toil and ceaseless tireless fight
With sullen apathy enthroned on high
Or blatant mob's blind brutal calumny.

Of these was he who found the people bent
Beneath a burden that they could not bear ;
Fair Commerce shackled stood, her strength o'er spent,
And all a-toss her sad dishevelled hair,—
He struck her bonds, the festering fetters broke—
An Empire leaped to greatness at the stroke.

High chieftain in our England's hero host,
Sure bladed captain in her postal fray,
We greet him silent on that silent coast
Where now he celebrates his natal day,—
And hail him where pale Progress' flag's unfurled
Dead mighty Midlander who shook the world.

Philatelic World, January 1896.

BRITANNIA'S SOLILOQUY, NO. 2.

(For No. 1, "On the new bronze Coinage" *vide* "Punch," 18th January [1896.)]

ONCE upon my Stamp was lined
Noble head of contour queenly ;
Now upon my Stamp I find
Vapid face that smirks serenely.
Then a regal head and grand
Simply graced each postal *billet*,
Now a paltry profile and
Lots of scrolls supremely silly.
Gracious me ! 'tis passing queer
Spite of Art's unceasing wooing—
Though the reign's demise is near
Still we stick to De-la-Rueing.

End the stuff! To Heath and Wyon
Who designed our earliest label
I'd revert the British Lion
Just as quick as I am able.

Philatelic World, March 1896.

RESIGNATION.

The Indian Post Office in order to attach the registration receipt form had at one time a habit of passing a thread through registered letters or packets regardless of the consequences to the contents. The protests of stamp collectors were long regarded with supreme indifference, but eventually the iniquitous custom was discontinued.

FOR the Law speaks sonorous and thrilling—
(So its settled and no-one asks why)
To the Post Office "cease not thy drilling!"
To the Custom House "pounce on and pry!"
Should a smart journalistical lancer
Deplore these here things in Bengal
We smile and we shrug as we answer
"Its the *hookhum* and *dustoor*—that's all.

Philatelic World, June 1896.

BRUSSELS SPROUTS.

THE ANTWERP EXHIBITION STAMPS.

ONE is mauve and
One is brown.
And in both the *devil's down.

Philatelic World, February, 1897.

SUGGESTED ARMS FOR THE PHILATELIC SOCIETY OF INDIA.

ARMS—(of pretension) QUARTERLY. First.—A Catalogue rouge or ruled quite on the square in full sale over a counter rampant urgent all passable.

---

* But perhaps the devil may be only a dragon after all.

Second.—A surcharge sable reversé issuant erased of small service barred (or Zanzibarred) spotted and exposed quite improper.

Third.—An album monstrant of assumption folioated garnished ruled and guarded inclined to become passé and warranted pucca under a protest.

Fourth.—A watermark gartered quadrillé or something of that sort out of repair and most depressé charged at with epithets all orful.

CREST.—A demi-seebeekulative gumbug prancеté embossed or otherwise habited gorgeous grilled and incorrect displayed all there on a field sanguine vert or azure under a cloud distinctive semisuppressed and held in check base most irregular.

SUPPORTER.—DEXTER. A magpie splendidus regardant and a trifle fretty on the pounce proper surfeited and gorged something dreadful.

SINISTER. A bloater fishant parti-coloured and shady, flaunted in rows on a pale of rectitude bordering on the secretly dotty denticulated at random 14½.

FIRST MOTTO. (Pregnant).—" Dum collecto spendo " (or words to that effect).

SECOND MOTTO.—" Quis sed stultus seperabit a tête bêche pair."

Philatelic World, March 1897.

A REJOINDER TO " MR. PUNCH."

(*See* " *Punch*," 15*th Oct.* 1898.)

(The Sage had immortalised in clever verse a suggestion to re-christen " Philatelists " " Philosemeiotisisiscomistographists.")

DESIST ! my Punch, avast ! belay !
  And also likewise drop it !
Hold hard ! avaunt that waggish way !
  My ancient friend do stop it !
Ye Muses, Fates, and Furies five—
  Ye Gods and Fish atomic—
Here's Fleet Street's Sage, as I'm alive,
  Indubitably comic ! !

Did I say five ?—It may be three—
(See Lempriére's columns frisky)
But pass the word to dear old P.
That funny verse is risky.
We can't afford to lose him yet—
So sober, staid, dejected :—
Wit hurts us bad because, you bet,
It's not what we expected.

" Ne Sutor ultra crep "—you know
The rest my stoic Nestor—
Stick to your last, for aye forego
The motley's luring vesture.
Leave frivol-fun and frolic-chaff
To them that knows the business—
Don't try again to make us laugh—
It leads to mutual dizziness.

We've laughed, we have, we've all avowed—
Your verse is turned so neatly—
Philosemiow—ow—ow—owed
So cat-like and so sweetly.
But most we laughed to hear you tell
Of one you were no funker—
But turned at last and went to—well
You must have missed the *punkha.*

"The Sage his page" soon resumed its scintillating brilliance after the above was rejoinded. It not long ago shone with a refulgent gleam from "Dâk" himself, the cutting sent being acknowledged by a card from the publishers and a copy of the paper, the personality of the contributor being kept da (r) k.

Philatelic Journal of India, December 1898.

THE "WIDOW" AGAIN.

[On the issue of the Indian 3 pies (carmine) of 1899.]

(*With the usual apologies.*)

MAKE way for the " Widow of Windsor,"
With the hairy gold crown on 'er 'ead
She's careering at large through the land of the Taj
A little old lady in red—
A delectable lady in red!

So room for the " Widow of Windsor,"
Our dainty Imperial Queen—
So neat and so nice at the cost of a *pice*
The " pink of perfection " serene.
(She's pink, but she used to be green) !
Hurrah for the " Widow of Windsor,"
O'er 'arf of our albums she's strewn—
For her court and her camp and her flag and her stamp
Have advancing ideas of their own—
Unique, but distinctly their own !

So we welcome this " Widow of Windsor,"
The least and the latest to come—
And it's true I dare say there are more on the way—
Then tune up the timbrel and drum—
We like 'em, so let 'em all come !

Philatelic Journal of India, February 1900.

SNIPPETS.

(From a review of the "American/"Australian Journal of Philately.")

THROUGH monthly brace of magazines the editorial scissors flit oh—
America has her " J. of P.," Australia has her ditto ditto,
'Twixt two such works o'er which to revel
'Tis hoped we 'll reach a worthy level.

" The overprint on the British North Borneo labels is in red or black, which is which does not matter."

Make your play gentlemen ! Red or Black ?
Mention your fancy then shuffle the pack !
Plank down your coppers ! We're been there before—
Red or Black, gentlemen ? *Rouge ou Noir ?*

Little marks of water, little dotlets (planned)
Make collectors callous—speculators grand.

The C. E. F. surcharges are now being freely forged.

There is a surcharge fair to see, Kubberdar!
A plain device of letters three, Kubberdar!
Trust it, yes, but not too far, Kubberdar!

Philatelic Journal of India, December, 1901.

DELHI.

On an expected new set of Indian stamps for the Delhi Durbar.

THEY are coming the stamps of the Kaiser-i-Hind;
Though they loiter a little we'll none of us mind
If they lend the light lustre of loyal *éclat*,
To that, dreamy delectable Delhi Durbar.

(But they did't come after all.)

Philatelic Journal of India, June, 1902.

PHANTOM FUN.

(*With the usual apologies*).

"Now we think it will be generally agreed that collectors find these so-called minor varieties an unmitigated nuisance."—MORLEY'S PHILATELIC JOURNAL.

A man there was and he made his prayer
(Even as you and I)
To a splash and a dash and a line of hair,
Or a sportive perf (he denoted it rare)—
For cover and card he had never a care
(Even as you and I.)

Oh the pipes we light and the cheques we write
In the spoil of the sea and land
Partake of the toll of the mean and small—
The fevered whim for the nothing-at-all—
One never can understand.

A man there was and his heart he bent—
(Even as you and I)
On fads and fakes to colossal extent—
(It wasn't a bit what Philately meant)
But the pigeon is plucked from Kabul to Kent
(Even as you and I.)

Oh the time we've lost and the cash it cost
On the wonderful stuff to hand—
On the crossless T and the dotless I—
And the phantom fun of a doubtful die
    We know it—and understand.

The man was sad when his purse was spent,
    (Even as you and I)
He fixed up an "ad," on a sale intent,
And sold—at a loss of some sixty per cent.;
(But that didn't matter so long as they went)
    (Even as you and I.)

Oh it isn't the price of the sacrifice
When we've furrowed the fruitless sand—
Its the fact of finding absurdity's marge
In the wild weird quest of the double surcharge
    That at last we understand.

Philatelic Journal of India, June 1902

THE WILES OF GREECE;

OR, WHAT NECKS?

"GREECE.—In a new design there is a profile of a young lady with Mercury's helmet and a very long neck. What the object of these may be, besides the raising of revenue from collectors we do not understand."—STANLEY GIBBONS' MONTHLY JOURNAL, *28th February* 1902.

THE stamps of Greece! The stamps of Greece!
    By Dorning Beckton loved and sung,
That won our hearts at school's release
E're Surcharge rose or Seebeck sprung!
Eternal wonder yields regret
At view of this the latest set.

The mountains look on Marathon.
And Marathon on LEΠ and ΔPA
But musing on the lot alone,
I wished the αλφα [illegible] away,—
And (guessing at the person's sex)
I could but deem them nerveless necks.

The "Paris" and the "Athens" prints,
The gracious poise of pinioned head,
The ample range of mellowed tints
And goodliest contours all are fled.—
Of stamps that stream from further west
They mind us most—unloved, unblest.

A King peers forth with racking brow
(Of Fuch's pen born—for sale amiss)
From stamps in thousands, row on row
Of many nations—all are his—
We count them spoil of Edward's day
Victoria's son's set—what are they?

Aye! what are they? And what has't thou
My Hellas! on thy labels rude?
The heroic face is vapid now—
The heroic glance obscure and crude,—
Why should that form so long divine
Degenerate to a weak design?

Thou hast the front of Hermes yet;
Where is the former Hermes gone?
Of two such models why forget
The earlier and the goodlier one?
Thou hast the letters Cadmus drew
A trifle blurred—a shade askew.

'Tis something mid the dearth of Art
Though living in Edwardian days—
To feel the true collector' s smart
E'en as I write suffuse my face.
For what is left collectors here?
For smile—a smirk. For grace—a smear.

Must we but grieve for days no more?
Must we despair the future's fame?
Art, yield us but from out thy store
A remnant of thy former flame.
In nineteen hundreds grant our plea
And make a new Philately.

What darkness near and darkness far?
Ah me, the works of Wyon dead
Loom mighty, mid the glare and jar
Of garrish green and ruddiest red!
The colours clash! The discords shriek!
'Tis but the dead who, silent, speak.

Too late—too late—smite other chords—
Fill high the page with Labuan's line!
Leave art to deck far Borneo's hordes—
Of ape and peacock large and fine—
To tap the flow of pence that fall
To them that leap to lucre's call.

Look not for light. Insipid Fuchs
Has made a King we buy and sell
Who, fronting gloom, the light rebukes
And likes the outlook all too well!
While specious fake and spacious fraud
O'er crowd our field however broad.

Fill high the page with Labuan's line!
Old Hellenes droop within the shade—
I mind their glorious lost dies' shine
While gazing on the growing trade
In apes the learning school-boy rules,
To think such beasts should suck-in fools!

Place me by Gibbons' marvellous page
And *purdha tarno*—none but I
May hear my muttered murmurous rage
As later listed Greeks go by.
The quest of these shall ne'er be mine
Shut down—shut down th' ignoble line!

Philatelic Journal of India, April 1902.

AFTER THE WAR-FLOOD.

ALL the world over
Counting his scars,
Stands the collector-man,
Bit by the wars.

Philatelic Journal of India, June 1902.

THOUGHTS AT A STAMP AUCTION.

TO right and left the seed was flung,
Till fields were red with waving grain—
Then down the great grim Hammer swung—
And others garner all his gain.

But yet 'twere well to call to mind,
Now all is said and dead and done—
He laughed if sowing to the wind,
Though others reap—he had his fun.

The quarry's quaint—the quest is good,—
To seek and sift and sort and see
Our harvest flush in rip'ning mood
Is gay good work for you and me.

Who reads herein knows all is right
Though Hammer fall—an ample creed,
He reaps who keeps the end in sight—
He lives who laughs and flings the seed.

Philatelic Journal of India, January, 1903.

PREFACE BY AN AD-INTERIM-EDITOR.*

"In the meanwhile we 'occur' with our usual unpunctuality.

WE chant the "Curzonation Set"
From Balliganj to Chili,
And babble of the gay *roulette*
And warble *en quadrille*.

We chatter, chatter as we go
By *dâk* to dusty Delhi—
Alive with clever terms you know
("Syllabic" or "burélé").

And chatter on in shining pars
Of "crescents," "curves" and "creases."
Of scintillating "Eastern Stars"
(With portrait frontispieces).†

---

* This writer, as usual, acted as editor of the *PHILATELIC JOURNAL OF INDIA* during an unavoidable editorial interregnum.

† A series of portraits of well-known Philatelists was appearing under the generic heading "Eastern Stars."

We snip and snipe, we chime and rhyme,—
We sparkle strong and steady—
We're hardly ever out to time,
Because we're seldom ready.

Of "die" and "dot" and "dash" and "dâk"
And weird "O. G." we rattle—
On many a wily "watermark,"
We turn our passing prattle.

We fume and fret at froward "fake"
That flouts us as we travel—
And talk of "Art for Art's own sake,"
(Like Walter Crane or Havell).

But none can mar and nought can jar,
All bad hap's unavailing—
What matters here, a big durbar—
Or there, a steamer's sailing?

We drub the postal-fiscal drum
With philatelic vigour—
For one may go or one may come,
But "we" go on for—as long as subscriptions continue to
    arrive.

Philatelic Journal of India, January 1903.

SERVIA.

The *Daily Mail* had reported that the new Servian stamps would have as their principal feature the Eagle of Servia and not a portrait of the new Ruler, Peter I.

A stricken King, bright blood-daubed silken curls,—
A raging world rings furious at the sight—
While sullen, whence the star-lit Danube swirls
An Eagle glares, red taloned, on the night.

Philatelic Journal of India, July 1903.

AN OLD SONG RE-SET.

"Look here upon this picture and on this,—
The counterfeit presentment of two *sisters*."

France.—"Two further values of 'the Sower' (*La Semeuse*) type have appeared."

Australian Commonwealth.—"The first Federal issue is chronicled."

THE lady from France she walks like this in a rousey manner,
The Sydney sort she sits like this in a drowsy manner,
Now which do you like the best, Good Sir,—
Now which do you like to see—
The crouching crude Australian girl—
Or the lady from gay Par-ee?

The lady from France she heralds the day in a breezy manner,
The other one shines in the grocery way in a cheesey manner,
Now which would you like to be, Madame,—
Now which would you like to be,—
The lightsome, lithe, Lutetian lass—
Or the maiden from far Sydn-ee?

The Parisian girl is frank and French in a cheery manner,
The grocery girl is a wearisome wench with a dreary manner.
So at whom shall we shout "a bas"! Monsieur?—
And for whom shall we shout "hurray"!?
For makeshift, muddling, Minister Drake?—
Or for Loubet and Delcassé?

Philatelic Journal of India, August 1903.

SING A SONG OF IMPRINTS.

"The practice is spreading of special issues for minute islands, &c., with, in some cases, about as many inhabitants as an ordinary house in London."

SING a song of Imprints
More or less awry—
What an opportunity
Now for printers' pie.

When the pie is sorted
  Then the islets sing
RURUTU and RAPA-TI—
  (That's the kind of thing).

Seddon from his counting house
  Spies an ocean-isle—
AITUTAKI, NIUE—
  (Shovel in the pile).

China-man he winkee,
  Makee muchee yen—
HOI-HAO, MONGTZE.
  PACKHOI, YUNNAN SEN.

Alfonso (Espana)
  Finds the plan to pay
ANNOBON, CORISCO.
  Also ELOBEY.

Pity poor Philately
  Sinking in her shame—
And may the Berne Bureau essay
  To stop the little game.

Philatelic Journal of India, September 1903.

THE VERY MAB.*

Why do these things happen? Perchance there is a Queen Mab of Philately of whom the modern Mercutio might tell us :—

This is that very Mab

TO dwarf the leaves of maple at the bend
  And cloud the light lines in thick sluttish hairs,
Which once engraven much misfortune yield.
This is the hag when stamps lie on the stocks
That tinkers them and earns them blame unfair
Making them issues of miscarriage—
This is the—

Philatelic Journal of India, September 1903.

*** (The approved design for new Canadian stamps had been greatly marred in the engraving.)**

TO THE FIRST SPANISH POSTAGE STAMP (1850).

"ISABELLA OF SPAIN IS DEAD."

QUAINT label, but it does seem strange to find
That there have passed some four and fifty seasons
Since first you loomed upon a world unkind—
For philatelic reasons.

Ah, what a world it was you fronted well,
What time she queened it over Don and Donna—
And what a lot has happed since Isabelle
Fled with dishonour.

They picked no holes in you, imperforate one,—
They picked them in Castile's imperious daughter,
Because at times the lady went and done
The which she didn't oughter.

We heard the shouts that rent the salvoed street
Acclaiming Prim a gallant people's head,
And flung with them our plaudits at his feet,—
For Isabelle had fled.

Crude label, since at first yon faced the day,
The folks we're apt to dub the "Latin Races"
Have caracoled a little in their way—
And shewn their paces.

Then mitred emblems graced the Papal *chits*
While you were young and Isabella blundered.
E'er Garibaldi blew their might to bits
When Cavour's cannon thundered.

Her morn was at the parting of the ways
That knew an elder order's waning power,—
And yet she lived to sound sleek Dumont's praise
Rounding the Eiffel Tower.

We shuddered oft to read of horrors fell
In dungeons foul 'neath glowing skies Sicilian
And cursed the lead that hissed the passing knell
Of kingly Maximilian.

Bomba and Bourbon all have reaped remorse
Since first you posed impassively platonic,—
And you have seen the full ill-fated course
Of things Napoleonic.

We mind a city steeled about for miles,
Begirt with flame and blood: we know the stories
Of an Imperial crowning at Versailles
  That clouded "All the Glories."

And when McKinley shuttered up that fleet
And laid the last least Spanish galleon low,
Hurling to Spanish pride a guerdon meet
  We joy'd that it was so.

And you who've weathered all the stirring file
Of six and thirty summers since she fled
Are here to tell she lived and loved awhile
  And now, at last, is dead.

Speak gently at her passing, veil her face,
Of royal stock she ruled a stubborn land—
Strong scion of the regal reigning race
  Of 'scutcheoned Ferdinand.

Ah, little stamp, would you could tell your mind,—
With what right pride a watchful world must prize you—
Great Gibbons!—after fifty years to find
  A penny buys you!!

Philatelic Journal of India, April, 1904.

A PLEASANT SURPRISE.

(*Gibbons' Stamp Weekly* had been announced to appear on 1st January 1905.)

COLLECTOR (enquiringly).

Dear me, what can the matter be?
What can the patter and chatter and clatter be
Now going on in the world of Philately
Going so strong in the air?

CHORUS OF RIVAL EDITORS.

They've promised to bring us a *weekly* new *Gibbons*—
They're going to spring on us another new *Gibbons*—
But they're not going to knock *our* concerns into ribbons
So we're none of us tearing our hair!

OMNES.

We're all of us in for another new *Gibbons*—
A whiff every week quite unique of our *Gibbons*—
And we'll fight for our bright little light, little, *Gibbons*—
The latest new thing in the air!

Philatelic Journal of India, October 1904.

MY OLD DUTCH.*

In the matter of perfs (the fault of the Dutch)
They're suppressing too little and printing too much.

Philatelic Journal of India, November 1904.

TÊTE BÊCHE; OR, ON A STRING.

IT was just when the War blundered out at the Cape
That I joined the concern of Tape Ticker and Tape,
I'd the shiniest hat with the brim all a-curl,
And just a suspicion of scorn for a girl.

We met at my aunt's, where she'd happened to call,
And I said "How-d'ye-doo-o?" in my easiest drawl.
She smiled—and at once I was hers to command
Without a suspicion of making a stand.

She'd the daintiest head with the daintiest poise,
And dimples that danced as delicious decoys;
Her laugh was a wonder, with gold in each note,
And she'd just a suspicion of lace at the throat.

Her gloves and her shoes were as neat as could be,
And her silk circled wrists quite refreshing to see,
She'd a veil that fell taut from a bright picture-hat,
And just a suspicion of scent and all that.

---

* About this time Mr. C. Stewart Wilson and other studious Philatelists were earnestly devoting much time and labour to the elucidation of the perforations of the stamps of Holland.

Well, I talked to the lady and happened to say
I was keen upon stamps in an amateur way;
She exclaimed, " let me see them, do, please, Mr. Jones !"
With the sweetest suspicion of zest in her tones.

" I dream about ' stamps,' though I've only a few
And, of course, my display will seem nothing to you;
And there's so much to learn I don't know that I ought—
I've a sort of suspicion I want to be taught."

So I showed her my stamps, and I showed my hand too,
When she glittered with glee o'er my best " Sydney View."
Saying " do, please, accept it! It's really quite good!"
Though I'd not a suspicion, of course, that she would.

But she did—and then kissed it with maidenly grace,
And glanced up her thanks from a down tilted face,
As she slipped the stamp into the belt at her waist,
And I'd just a suspicion that kiss was misplaced.

Well, that was the start, though the end isn't yet,
For her teeth are still pearls, and her locks are still jet,
When we met and I " parted " I learned to be schooled
To the gentle suspicion, " It's nice to be fooled."

Her album waxed bulky as my album waned,
For we knew how to fill in the time when it rained;
And my aunt used to smile from her knitting anon
Without a suspicion of all that was on.

It happened the year that Victoria died
That she flashed down an aisle as a bride at my side;
As an " unsevered pair " we have journeyed since then
Without a suspicion of cloud in our ken.

It happened last week, though, I thought I'd go back
To the pleasure-decked charm of Philately's track;
I looked for our albums, and—(here a bad word)—
Though I'd not a suspicion of what had occurred.

She mused. " Stamps ? Oh, its Stamps I suppose you must mean"
(With a far away look and a gesture serene).
" Why, I've threaded them on to a string for Tom's sake,
And he hugs the suspicion they must be a snake."

" The dear little fellow, he screams with delight
When it wriggles about in his bath-tub at night;
He tickles his toes with the slimy affair,
With the leastest suspicion of fear in his air."

I observed " Oh, indeed !" and the dear little chap
Crowed " Vevvy big snake !" from his fair mother's lap,
But, as I had really small cause to rejoice,
There was just a suspicion of doubt in my voice.

Then she pouted and, tossing her picturesque head,
Said, " I'm going to collect picture-postcards instead,
I think picture-postcards are nicer by far "—
And I'd quite a suspicion I'd met with a jar.

Then they skipped round the room in an improvised waltz,
And I pardoned the snake on the spot for his faults;
For I couldn't be harsh with my darling for long,
Though I've still a suspicion my darling was wrong.

Gibbons' Stamp Weekly, 1*st April* 1905.

THE RUSSIAN WAR STAMPS.

LEAVE the Eagle Flag a-flying just awhile, and shrieve the dying—
Drub the drum and bid the fifes their tidings call—
From the shattered bastions' massing they are passing, passing, passing
To the glory that awaits beyond the wall.

Famine-faint and fever-haunted, grim and gaunt, but heart undaunted,
They are marching, marching, marching out elate;
For the wan worn warriors brighten and the war-scarred faces lighten
To the cheers for gallant Stoessel in his passage through the gate.

There's a shuttered palace groaning, there are wind-swept streets a-moaning
(God ! the girls and little children that are there !);
For the maxims are a-calling—Ah ! they're falling, falling, falling
To the rush of steel-shod squadrons in the square !

" Little Father !" they are crying, " Little Father we are dying !
We are dying for the land we love and thee !"
But the silence is unbroken and the word remains unspoken
From the shuttered palace sobbing for the peoples still unfree.

I hate to preach and pester—I who pose a motleyed jester—
But a jester has his message clear and shrill,—
There is sorrow, sorrow, sorrow all to-day and each to-morrow
Which all of us can lessen if we will.

Let the Czar of every Russia ne'er attempt again to crush a
Right upheaval of his people straight and true.
And may the Russian nations never cease their protestations
While regardful of their monarch and their monarch's point of view.

And may you and I, my readers, constitute ourselves the pleaders
For the labels that a stricken folk have planned—
Little shuttles trailing glory as they flash the sacred story
Of the love that speaks no language and that knows no creed or land.

Gibbons' Stamp Weekly, 8th April 1905.

FANCY DRESS.

(Spain had issued Cervantes Commemoration stamps depicting incidents in the career of Don Quixote.)

With apologies to the producers of "The Orchid" at the Gaiety Theatre.

ENGLAND: Fancy me with a fancy set—
But not just yet—
CHORUS: Not just yet.
ENGLAND: I'd re-illumine a household pet
From the page of a popular story;—
What's the matter with Dan Defoe?
I don't know—
CHORUS: We don't know.
ENGLAND: So limelight, please, for our R. Crusoe
Aglow with Philately's glory!
Only fancy, fancy, me
Booming robust old Robinson C.!
Wouldn't he just be all the rage
Neatly perf'd to a regular gauge?
ENGLAND: Or I might show you a sprightly dame,
Known to fame—
CHORUS: Known to fame.

ENGLAND: I can't at the moment recall her name,
But she pranced with a white horse under;
She'd have rings on her fingers too—
Bells at shoe—
CHORUS: Bells at shoe—
ENGLAND: And I'd catalogue her (by De La Rue)
As Philately's latest wonder.
Only fancy, don't mistake,
Wouldn't she take the Banbury cake?
And wouldn't it just be nice to see
Her steed nicknamed "the original G"?
FRANCE: I've a wonderful writing star—
Great Dumas!
CHORUS: Grand Dumas!
FRANCE: I've an idea he outshines by far
The rest of romantic writers.
How collectors would all shell out—
There's no doubt!
CHORUS: Not a doubt!
FRANCE: For a "rainbow" set that was all about
His rollicking, roystering fighters.
Only think how the world would stare
At a nice little lot from Les Mosquetaires—
Oh, wouldn't they knock our friend Don Q.
In the pictured page of S. G., Part II?
Only fancy that wonderful leap
To the bleak, black depths from the chateau'd steep,
And think of the splash in the rushing dark
As suggestive at least of a water-mark.
AUSTRIA: There's a work that I fancy well,—
Shall I tell?
CHORUS: Please, do tell!
AUSTRIA: Its all of us held 'neath a lasting spell,
And is known as the "Strewelpeter."
I'd have stamps to depict its verse—
I might do worse!
CHORUS: You might do worse!
'T would help to replenish the national purse
And render success completer!
Only fancy, when I get
My "Great Agrippa" or "Greenman" set,
And think of the grist that would come to my mill
From the sale of (inverted) "Fidgety Phil."

PERSIA: I'm for a lot in a different line—
Roses and wine!
CHORUS: Bright sunshine!
PERSIA: A loaf and a jug and a "Thou" divine
And everything Omar Kyammy.
It would be certain to come to stay,
Quite *au fait!*
CHORUS: Quite "O. K."!
PERSIA: As something serene in a lotus-like way,
Gentle and jolly and jammy.
Only fancy, fancy me
Loving and laughing under a tree—
Lolling at ease through a golden noon
Heedless that all would be ended soon.
U. S. A.: I'd have stamps in a novel dress
Yus, I guess—
CHORUS: Yus, we guess—
U. S. A.: Parad and puffed in the daily Press;
With big brass bands to foller;
Say, theer, stranger, what d'yer think
Of Rip Van Wink.
CHORUS: (Ah, Rip Van Wink!)
U. S. A.: As a striking assortment in aniline ink
Asnore in his Sleepy Holler?
Fancy me wheer the Katskills loom,
Manipulatin' a Winkle boom
In Philately's name with a capital P—
You bet I'd embody *le dernier cri.*
ALL: Ah, fancy us on the Spaniard's tack!
With stack and pack,
Pack and stack.
Of our own Don Q's to get each our whack
For the golden flow a-racing!
But don't suppose we mean what we say
Ah, no, nay! Ah, no, nay!
We're not such fools, in a general way,
As to go such a wild-goose chasing.

Gibbons' Stamp Weekly, 17*th June,* 1905.

PHI-LEAR-TELIC LIMERICKS.

With apologies to the shade of the late Edward Lear,—prince of Nonsense rhymers.

" Egyptian stamps, you may sware-o "
" Come straight from the land of Pharaoh "
" They're got up in style "
" On the banks of the Nile— "
" Rectangular, oval, and square-o "

Prehistoric philatelic,—(*Circa the mid-sixties*)

SAID the Penny (Type 1) of Antigua
To the Five Shillings (5), "Why how big you are!
Who replied, " Oh, my ' Queen,'
Is it size that you mean ?
Or do you refer to my figua ?"

The unannexed land of Nepal
Said, " I can't understand it at all
Why, I'm catalogued straight
As an Indian State
By Gibbons, by Scott, and by all."

Said the short-listed State of Sirmoor
(Though longer than Bhundi or Bhore),
" You must lengthen my list—
Come you must, I insist—
Sir (Moor) Masson's discovered some more."

An African island Mauritius,
Vexed us all with surcharging capricious;
But the " Star and the Key
Of the Indian Sea "
Has turned from the way that is vicious.

A wise little island Hongkong,
Thinks change without reason is wrong;
With a dainty design—
Neat effective, and fine—
She has charmed the whole world all along.

The earliest issue of Ind
Were the circular trio of Scinde,
By Sir Bartle embossed,
At a trifling cost
For the purpose of raising the wind.

To the popular ruler of Spain
We've carolled this eloquent strain—
"We're all of us gloaty
On dear Don Quixote,
But, please, never do it again."

The Papal emissions of Rome
Passed away like the spray of the foam—
All *les timbres de l'eglise*
(With the Mitre and Keys)
When Nap wanted bayonets at home.

The issues of Australeear
Have declined very much below par.
Till one's quite at a loss,
'Neath the gay Southern Cross,
To exactly quite know where he are.

They had a big show in Bruxelles,
And invented some labels to sell;
In both violet and brown
The old devil is down,
And, of course, on the whole it's as well.

The Lady from France, "La Semeuse"
(All alive and alert like Chartreuse).
Is *le dernier cri*
(The delectable She)
From her *chapeau en rouge* to her shoes.

When will France (*a la* Madame Tussaud)
Show her rulers on stamps in a row—
McMahon, Loubet,
Casimir-Perier,
Thiers, Grevy, F. Faure, and Carnot?

Poor Russia is nearly distraught
(I wouldn't reside at her Court),
But I think you'll agree
With my judgment that she
Has stamps that are gems of a sort.

There was a bold King of Siam
(Not the birthland of Omar Khayyam)
Who delighted the flats
With assortments of Atts,
And remarked, " What a brave boy I am."

On a holiday bent, said his *frau*
To Herr Schmidt,
" Why not try Kiauchou ? "
Who replied " Yes, my dear,
Why we will—if its near !"
(But they've not been there yet, anyhow).

The " blocks " of Cap Bonne-Esperance
(That's the name that it's known by in France)
Were purchased in sacks
(Brought by tars on their backs)
By Gibbons, who started to prauce.

The current I ΔRAKMAI wakes one's
Misgivings, lest Hellas' fine sons,
In their fervour for fame,
Overtrained and went lame
And were known as the " O'limpy-uns."

The medal-like stamps of Lagos
Fell victims to cheapness, because
That curse of the day
Swept the beauties away,
And they was so delightful—they was

I've gone a bit wrong, for I find
I had Gambian stamps in my mind
When I wrote the last verse
On Philately's curse
(Perhaps I'd but recently dined).

In the stamps of the land of King Haakon
More interest now will be taaken,
You can all go and see 'em
At the British Museum,
Neatly mounted by E. Denny Baacon.

There's a wild woolly beast of Peru.
(Rouletted, dos centavos, blue);
This Lama of Lima
Is worthy a rhymer
Who'd tip him a canto or two.

Some stamps of the Etats-Unis
(That's the land of "the blest and the free")
Have corners and frills,
Frames, centres, and *grilles*—
All a bit of a puzzle to me.

The lady-like issues of Nevis
In all of our hearts found a niche.
When he said, "Are they cheap?"
They replied, "No, they're not!"
Vita brevis, but art it is longer.

Of the States of the great Hindustan,
I'm completest in that of Wadhwan.
Hullo! What's this? I say,
Why the stamp's blown away!
(It must have been done by the fan).

Said the stamps of the State Sarawak
To those of Malayan Perak,
"If we let our 'K's go,
Like the 'K' in Bangkok,
We shall thrive with the clearer *éclat*."

The Afghans are black-bearded folks
Who come to Calcutta with mokes
Piled with Shere Ali sets,
And black kittens for pets,
Which they swap—but they've knives up their cloaks.

Of frauds I could sing you a song,
Like Sedangs, which are wrong, very wrong,
Some day we may get
A debatable set
From "the beautiful valley of Bhong."

Gibbons' Stamp Weekly, *17th November* 1906.

POSTPONED.

"Visitors to the Minto Fête will regret to learn that the stamp exhibition arranged for by the Philatelic Society of India has been postponed. *The stamps received and promised are so numerous and valuable that it was felt that the management would not be justified in holding the display on the *Maidan*, the more so as the tent provided would have proved too small for the exhibits.

Our local philatelic friends are to be congratulated on escaping a succession of sleepless nights. The exhibition as at first planned for would have been a nerve-shaking arrangement.—*The Empire.*

TO be, or not to be,—that is the question :—
Whether 'tis better to be blind and suffer
The things that harrow with benumbing caution,
Stifle alarms, and risk a sea of troubles,
Or, by postponing, end them ? To try to sleep,—
O lor ! and if to sleep to think we end
The headache and the philatelic shocks
We might be heir to,—'tis a calculation
Discreetly to be missed. To try to sleep ;—
To sleep ! perchance to dream :—ay, there's the rub ;
For in that sleep, some night, what things might come,
Did we not hasten out of all this toil
Must give us pause : there's an effect
That makes calamity of any life ;
For who would bear the ups and downs of chance,
The fireman's gong, the scoffer's contumely,
The Ochterlony backed by flames' array,
The "there I told you so's," and all the spurns
That mildew, fire or tempest-torments bring,
When each himself might his '*quietus*' make
With a bare put off ? Who would badges wear
To work and watch over a worried week,
Filled with the dread of something all the while,—
An all impending horror from whose clutch
Collections ne'er return,—puzzles the will,
And makes us rather bear the nerves we have
Than make for others we can well wot of ?
Thus caution doth make laggards of us all ;
And leads us on to frame a resolution
Resultant of belated after-thought ;
Our enterprise of pith, just for the moment,
(With this regard, its current turned away)
Casts off the thought of action.
The Empire, 30th January 1907.

---

* H. R. H. the Prince of Wales sent a magnificent selection from his own collection.

WHICH ?

"BARBADOS" or "Barbadoes"
Which ? who is there known who knows ?
And yet somehow the mind it poses
To think of the plural as "Barbadoses."

Philatelic Journal of India, February 1907.

ONCE MOORE.

A one-time worshipper of the "vertical hyphen and the dotless i" wails as follows :—

"THE time I've lost in viewing,
In watching, and pursuing
The fun, that lies in dotless i's
Has been my time's undoing.
Though fiscals oft have sought me,
I scorned the lore they brought me,
My only stamps
Where freaks and vamps—
And folly's all they've taught me."

Philatelic Journal of India, February 1907.

THE BABY, THE PUP, AND THE BUNNY.

There is an absurdity going the rounds of the press with a crowd of parodies in its wake. No apology is made for the following, it was bound to come, let's get it over.

THE brave bâtonné Baby and the Philatelic Pup
Were playing in the compound when the Bunny ambled up ;
They looked upon the surcharge with a loathing undisguised
It wasn't perforated and it wasn't fiscalised.
They said it was quadrillé and a hair-line of disease,.
And they steamed it in burélé of uncatalogued degrees.
They twirled it in a tweezer that was cold as safety rum,
And washed it in an aniline of mercury and gum.
In marginal syllabics they engraved its granite flaps,
And hinged its plated matrix to a lower-case of caps.
They donned their tête bêche watermarks and took it by the hand,
And elected it an Album of the Unrouletted Band.
There isn't a remainder in the compound where they play ;
They float in purest benzine for a dozen times a day ;
And each can gauge his metre from a typographic cup—
The Bunny and the Baby and the Philatelic Pup.

Philatelic Journal of India, February 1907.

AY, THERE'S THE RUB.*

A London paper's christened me
"The Laureate of Philately."
It's very nice when people praise
One's trivial imitative lays
I didn't know poetic fire
Inspired my philatelic lyre.
They say it does, so we'll suppose
Them right, and once again—here goes.
(This sort of thing, 'twixt you and I
Is very easy when you try.)

CHALKEE, or not Chalkee, that is the question:
Whether 'tis better, though half blind, to suffer
The things that harrow with courageous caution
Or to take care to never see our troubles,
And, by neglecting, end them? To buy,—to keep
(Oh lor); and, if to keep, to think we end
The headache (plus the other actual shocks)
The cult is heir to. 'Tis a consummation
Demurely to be dished. To buy,—to keep,—
To rub a surfaced ream;—ay, there's the rub;
For if we keep them all, what work will come
This gives us pause: there's the respect
That makes calamity of half our life:
For who would bear the work and waste of time,
The mocker's wrong, the sane man's contumely,
The gibe "Cornelius" loves in wrinkled way,
The insolence of others, and the spurns
That patient study of th' unworthy takes,
Should he himself essay the smirchment made
With a bare sixpence? Who for these things would care
To frown and sweat a philatelic life,
Did he not fear lest issues afterwards
(Of some new listed country) yet unborn,
Make Gibbons turn?—puzzles our will
And makes us rather hate the stamps we have
And cry for Chalkees that we know not of?
For fashion doth make turncoats of us all.
And when the native hue of our collection

*** The question of specially listing chalk-surfaced stamps in catalogues and albums was to the front. Chalk on a stamp may be detected by rubbing it with a silver coin.**

Is silvered o'er with a pale smudge of chalk
'Twere not surprising then, on spur of moment,
Did we regard stamps current all awry
And loose the same to auction.

Gibbons' Stamp Weekly, 16*th February* 1907.

I REMEMBER, I REMEMBER.

(*With apologies to the shade of Hood.*)

I remember, I remember,
The house where I was born,
The little album where the stamps
Were peeped upon at morn;
They never seemed a bit too torn
Or chipped too much that day,
But now the slightest scratch or crease
Takes all the charm away!

I remember, I remember,
The British red and blue,
The Perkins and the Bacons
And the gems of De-la-Rue?
The Hongkong my dead brother gave
To start my earliest set—
'T was laburnum—on my birthday—
(That Hongkong's living yet).

I remember, I remember,
The shop I used to know,
The little window hung with stamps
O'er forty years ago.
My pennies flew in feathers then
(I call them sovereigns now);
And play or school could never cool
The fever on my brow.

I remember, I remember,
The prices I thought high;
I used to think that eighteen pence
Was close against the sky.
It was a childish ignorance
But now 'tis little joy
To know I'm further off some stamps
Than when I was a boy.

Gibbons' Stamp Weekly, 7*th December* 1907.

TO STANLEY GIBBONS' "MONTHLY JOURNAL."

(1*st July* 1890—30*th June* 1908.)

On its decease to make way for "Gibbons' Stamp Weekly."

WELL done! old friend, well done! well done!
We greet you, passing in your strength—
Your strenuous course right royally run
Through all its length.

We mind you in those early years,
As now in these of riper time
Smiter of wrong, devoid of fears,
As in your prime.

You've helped Collecting on its way
With cheery will and skill surprising,
And emphasized its gracious sway
So humanizing.

And we shall miss you when you're stilled;—
Not one of your now crowded stage
Can quite assume the place long filled
By your bright page.

Well gauged, well centred, well impressed,
Well issued, you've fulfilled your mission,
And bravely stood the standard test
Of Mint Condition.

Strong king of your delightful kind,
Sage of our cult the wide world through,
The Nestor of your school and mind,
Our thanks to you—

Our thanks to him* who, rightly placed,
Planned you with intuition fine,
Whose gentle golden pen has graced
Each line on line.

---

* Major Edward B. Evans.

With other days come other ways,
And other men bring other manners,
And all must serve in coming days
'Neath other banners.

But you, 'spite years of wear and tear,
Easily first, *the* monthly journal,
Will ever rank with things that bear
A stamp eternal.

For you are of the stuff that lives,
The stuff that tells—to-day, to-morrow,—
Of proven mettle such that gives
No cause for sorrow.

And so farewell, our veteran wise,
Wreathed with the crown that worth enticeth,
We joy you'll come in newer guise,
And it sufficeth—

To know that through the days unborn,
In wisdom's ways with sweet beguiling,
You'll lead us still with strength unshorn,
And turn up smiling—

Turn up each week with kindly face
And truthful aim and ample pages,
And run anew a goodly race
Down through the ages.

The Monthly Journal, 30th June 1908.*

*** With these verses the long and illustrious career of the most distinguished of all the English philatelic periodical publications was brought to a close.**

Uniform with the present volume.

"DÂK DICTA."

BY

WILMOT CORFIELD ("DÂK").

CALCUTTA. THACKER, SPINK & CO. Rupees THREE.

The Empire, 19th November 1910.—We understand that the verses by "Dâk" in honour of H. E. Lord Minto, which appeared in the *Empire* of the 30th March last, at the foot of a cartoon by Mr. Frank Leah, have found their way to Canada, where they may be seen framed and hung up in the vestibule of the Ottawa Club.

The Journal, 20th November 1910.—The greatest event of the coming week, if the coming Viceroy will pardon us for saying so, will not be the appearance of Lord Hardinge but of "Dâk Dicta." Viceroys may come and Viceroys may go, but "Dâk" goes on for ever * * *. His is a pretty stream at once sportive and beautiful, never tired and never tiring. He passes through scenery the most diversified, fair women and brave men linger on his banks, and he delights to bicker on old abbeys, stately homes, and pleasant country paths. His music is never out of place nor out of tune, unless it is so intentionally, for our poet has an abiding humour. "Dâk Dicta" is a collection of poems grave and gay, songs sung by the way, which we venture to predict will be even more popular than the "Obiter Dicta" of the worthy Mr. Birrell. It will be published to-morrow by the famous firm of Messrs. Thacker, Spink & Co., its price, rupees three. But nothing can be too dear to the book lover and 'Dâk'" is dear to us all.

The Englishman, 25th November 1910.—Dâk presented a beautifully bound copy of "Dâk Dicta" to Lord Minto as a farewell gift and one of the last things his lordship did before leaving Calcutta was to write a charming letter of thanks in the course of which he declared himself "a great admirer of "Dâk."

The Journal, 27th November 1910.—The latest volume from our local bard has burst upon an admiring world, and should go far to enhance a fame already considerable. We take a *special* pride in the fact that these poems have all, without exception, been written in Calcutta. Many of them have seen the light already in the pages of this *Journal* and of local contemporaries. But "the reading that has pleased will please again," and there are many that will be glad to renew acquaintance with such things of beauty as "Missing" and "Found," "Edyth," "The Lilac Aisle," "Shadowland" and the touching lines on Thackeray. These are of the stuff that endures. But there are other pieces equally good in their way, verses on "Job Charnock" and on Bengal politics (the latter indeed may gain in value as the years go by), on elephants, dhobies and fakirs. The volume is spiced with humour and shows the poet in his every mood * * "Dâk" is a man of many sympathies, and his "Dicta" should appeal to a wide audience. Messrs. Thacker, Spink & Co. are to be congratulated upon the enshrining volume, artistic and original in design. A word in conclusion. We recommend everyone to read the preface, more interesting than prefaces generally are, and we venture to think that the portrait with which the volume opens will steal the reader's heart straight away and make him a kindlier critic and a still warmer admirer of the leading poet of Calcutta.

The Englishman 28th November 1910.—"Dâk" is a familiar name to readers of the *Englishman*, and especially to readers of these particular (the "Reviews of Books") columns. Admirers of his poetry, and they are legion in Calcutta, will welcome the republication of his verses in a neat volume.* * "Dâk Dicta" should command a large sale in this city of which its author might be called the laureate. "Dâk's" style is Kiplingesque in wealth of oriental colour and swinging melody of line. There is no style more difficult than Kipling's to follow without incurring the liability of being called a copyist. But "Dâk" is far from being a copyist in the sense that his work is not original. He is a clever parodist * * * but distinctly a poet with a poet's imagination and insight and a poet's range of vivid language. and he has besides that saving quality of humour and the power to express it in verse rare in poets. Take as a sample of his humour "The song of the Elephants" in which he tries to reproduce in —— verse the song and the stride of an elephant. But we like best of all the pieces in which "Dâk" strikes the loftier note of Patriotism and Imperialism. His verse tingles with pride at the recollection of British valour, and he has the power to express it with vivid colouring and force. Listen to this. (Quotes.) There are other verses, vigorous moving poetry reflecting the grandeur of the East and the leaping flame of patriotism. Listen again to this vibrant chronicle of the heroes of Indian history whose statues adorn Calcutta. (Quotes.) This most readable book should find a place in all libraries, and although "Dâk" tells us he is retiring from India. * * * * we hope India will see a good deal yet of the products of his ready pen and vigorous muse.

The Asian, 26th November 1910.—"Dâk Dicta" has now been issued and is already in so much demand that a second edition will probably shortly be called for. The book, a really sumptuous volume and a credit to the publishers, Messrs. Thacker, Spink & Co., is full of good things * * on all sorts of topics served up in "Dâk's" well-known trenchant style. * * A preface gives an interesting insight into the varied journalistic experiences of the author.

The Empire, 3rd December 1910.—Among the Anglo-Indian poets of to-day Mr. Wilmot Corfield ("Dâk") occupies a very high place. In his verses there is no straining after effect, no juggling with words, and no vulgarity. In his recently published volume, "Dâk Dicta," Mr. Corfield has fully maintained his reputation as a poet of a very high class. Some of his poems no doubt smack of the hour, but even a hasty glance at them will shew their great merit. His "Dicta" contains a selection of verses contributed by him to the *Empire* and other newspapers and magazines during the last four years. We strongly recommend our readers to purchase his "Dicta" and can confidently say they will not make a bad investment. We congratulate Messrs. Thacker, Spink & Co. on its excellent printing and get up.

The Indian Daily News, 9th December 1910.—*A notable book of verse.* It is not surprising that Mr. Wilmot Corfield's book of verse has already sold out its first edition, and that a second is in course of preparation for " Dâk " is quite one of the most tuneful Anglo-Indian versifiers of the last quarter century, and his mastery of words and the technique of his craft are evident on every page of the present volume. The experiment of republishing what is called in newspaper slang "occasional" verse is always somewhat risky. Written for particular incidents and occasions, it seldom stands the test of resurrection in a more permanent form. It says something for the quality of Mr. Corfield's poems that they will stand the test most successfully. Such pieces as " Plassey," " The Chapel at the Bay," and " By the Red Tank," to mention a few only read with fine lilt and swing. Perhaps in some of the verses the colour is laid on too thickly, and the adjectives riot with tropical luxuriance, but the best point is the absence of those painful breaks in the rhythm and mis-rhyming, which spoil most Anglo-Indian verses, except those of the very best—Kipling and Laurence Hope.

So much for praise. But the reviewer cannot conceal the fact that several of Mr. Corfield's poems and the tone of many more have caused him a certain deep-seated pain, for " Dâk " is a very violent politician indeed: the reviewer also, but on the other side. In his early years at Birmingham " Dâk " has confessed to a fierce uncompromising Radicalism. There is at present about as much Radicalism in his muse as there is in the opinions of that other Birmingham product Mr. Joseph Chamberlain. As a result the feelings of the loyal follower of Mr. Asquith in reading the " Dicta " resemble the feelings of an Archbishop of Canterbury condemned fifty years ago to read the early poems of Algernon Charles Swinburne, the only Englishman who knew how to " epater les bourgeois " if the " bourgeois " had been in the habit of reading poetry. But since they were not, they were not then (nor as yet now) in any way " epates." Mr. Corfield has a fine contempt for Mr. William Watson and others of similar views. But for all that there is a new Imperialism on the way which will be finer and broader than the old without falling into the mistake that some people may occasionally have made that their own country was always in the wrong. When it does come it might engage the attention of " Dâk " and afford him an opportunity of amalgamating his old and present self and enable him to produce a volume of verse of equal technical excellence with the present, but with a wider area of appeal than some of the verses included in the " Dicta " possess.

Commerce, 14th December 1910.—I have been reading with very great interest and entertainment, Mr. Wilmot Corfield's nicely got up volume of collected verses which Messrs. Thacker, Spink & Co. have issued from their press. " Dâk Dicta " is as good as its title is happy. It has been an open secret for some time that " Dâk," the witty versifier who has so often satirised or immortalised local doings and sayings was identical with the philatelist, accountant and historical society devotee who has audited so many ledgers in Calcutta. The city is to be congratulated upon producing so notable a poet from among its business men. I understand that Mr. Corfield is retiring and that he will shortly proceed to England, as he is still a young man, a great many busy and prosperous years are, I trust, in store for him.

Bengal: Past and Present, December 1910.—As many of the verses which make up this pleasant volume have appeared in *Bengal: Past and Present*, it would be but praising our own wares to review them in this place, and we must restrict ourselves to recommending the book to our readers. Mr. Corfield has a fine sense of the picturesque in Anglo-Bengal history and a mastery of the language appropriate to his subject. The lines on Murshidabad seem to us to have exactly caught the sentiment of the " Crumbled Courts of Murshed." Mr. Corfield, it must be admitted, is far too fond of some bad old historical myths and he stretches the poet's license rather far when he suggests that Job Charnock may perhaps have listened to the preaching of John Bunyan which seems to have commenced about the time Calcutta's founder arrived in Bengal. It is on record that Job arrived with Cavalier locks floating over his shoulders, and that his head was shorn as a concession to the prejudices of "the Moors." We do not for one moment incline to the suggestion that old Job ever entertained a tender regard for puritans or puritanism. Perhaps Mr. Corfield will at some time conjure up the Cavalier Job Charnock haunted at times by a devotion to lost causes and impossible loyalties, but above all a clear-sighted Yorkshireman. We commend "Dâk Dicta" most heartily. Mr. Corfield has been Treasurer of the Historical Society since its first formation and has done Yeoman's service in the cause we have at heart. In bidding him farewell on the occasion of his retirement from India, we console ourselves with the reflection that there will be plenty of work for him to do for us in the homeland, and we look to him to illustrate the maxim of his favourite Horace—"Cœlum, non animum mutant, qui trans mare currunt."—W. K. F.

The Planters' Gazette, 17th December 1910.—Talking of verses recalls the fact that I owe a very large measure of thanks to Mr. Wilmot Corfield for a copy of his "Dâk Dicta."

Dicita, Dicita Dâk,
The Muse began to ták.

It is terribly catching, but it does not come as easily to me as it does to "Dâk." As a matter of fact I have only driven my string-halt Pegasus into a blundering three-legged canter because "Dâk" set the fashion of reviewing books in verse, and because I had been reading his excellent poems that forced high praise from Lord Minto. If my verse is rough, and halting—well I am no bard, no Dâk ter of music.

The Indian Daily Telegraph, 24th December 1910.—Mr. Wilmot Corfield holds a distinguished place among Anglo-Indian poets. He has recently collected and published in book form, through Messrs. Thacker, Spink & Co., Calcutta, various of his contributions to the Press, and there is hardly one among them that does not deserve a place in the handsome volume "Dâk Dicta," all possessing the quality which recommends such compositions to the public—smooth numbers. "Clive and England! Clive and Empire!" is a stirring poem, also "Sons of the Flag," which reminds one of Kipling. The Author is well versed in Hindu mythology, and in many of his verses he introduced gods and sages of India's past, such as in the "Fakir," "The Maker of Gods,' etc. Among his satirical verses, one might mention "The Other Bomb" on Mr. Chuckerbutty's reply to the Court in the Bomb trial, that the bomb found on 31st July was like the other bomb, and the poet asks: "But if t'other's like the other, why then what's the other like?"

The Rangoon Times, 24th December 1910.—"Dâk Dicta" (Thacker, Spink & Co., Calcutta) contains a selection from verses written in Calcutta during the years 1907 to 1910 by one who was well known to readers of *The Englishman* and *The Empire* by his nom-de-plume of "Dâk." Scarce a morning's issue of *The Englishman* appeared without a contribution by "Dâk" in the form of a review of the latest book or a comment on passing events—comment strong with British sense and a *sahib's* way of thought, that came like a breath of fresh air into the atmosphere of Indian politics. Refreshing our memory from "Dâk Dicta," we seem to see, in this review of the last four years, John Bull is dozing—the true spirit of the race lies dormant, and, meanwhile, those lesser beings that infest the British Empire are emboldened to indulge in apish frolics, unrestrained; schoolboy seditionists, sloppy orators, Bengali heroes, women suffragettes, and all the rag-tag of politicians fill the arena and monopolise the attention of the public by their noisy chatter. John Bull is dozing, and when roused by the importunity of their demands.

"With pushful haste we give, and turn to snore;
The more we give, the cry goes up for more,
Not one will thank us of the clamant band,
And when we wake, 'twill be beyond the door."

So says "Dâk." Would that "Dâk" had found more time to voice the humour of the *Sahiblog* and to prick with his firm-grasped pen the frothy agitation that bubbled to the surface of that cauldron of self-stirred discontent, Calcutta,

"Where the great city of amorphous aim.
Its sad sore crown of self-wrought sorrow wears."

The bubble of the Maniktollah conspiracy burst at length; and its absurdity was disclosed when the scene of action was removed to the law-courts, a battle field less dangerous for the skins of the pleader seditionists. But possibly the surface of Indian life would have been less sullied if the movement, in its early stages, had been publicly treated with the humorous contempt with which it was regarded by the genuine Britisher.

We need more men like "Dâk," and it is with great regret that we gather, from the last poem of this collection, that its author, Mr. Wilmot Corfield, is about to retire from India "after residence in Calcutta during the eight Viceroyalties of Lords Dufferin, Lansdowne, Elgin, Curzon, Ampthill, Curzon, Minto and Hardinge."

We hope that "Dâk," in his retirement in England, may still be of service to us and boldly repeat,

"What India needs is British rule—no blend,
Pure undiluted Rule of British brew;
Preach that, Macdonald man, misguiding friend,
Or dry up, do."

The Times of India.—Light verse that is at all good is so rare an accomplishment that a ready welcome should be assured to the two writers who have established a reputation in India, "Dum Dum" (John Kendall) and Mr. Wilmot Corfield. Mr. Corfield's work reaches a high level. The following Tour-de-force is typical and may be quoted:—

"Proud sons of England, sires of England's sword,
Ere yet they donned the spurs of gold for fray
Naked a knight before an altar'd Lord
Swore fealty in an earlier knightlier day.
He who the throne of purple East would fill
Unseen may seek at God's high wisdom'd feet
Right turned at heart, His purposes high to will
Selfless to kneel at Heaven's white mercy seat
Thus strengthen'd rise for service all complete."

The Statesman, 25th January 1911.—The selection from verses written by Mr. Wilmot Corfield which has been published by Messrs. Thacker, Spink & Co., under the title of "Dâk Dicta" is of especial interest to Calcutta readers. Mr. Corfield is, of course, a politician of strong views, and those who do not see with his eyes will doubtless find little pleasure in his political rhymes. But allowance must be made for poetic licence, and besides many of the verses deal with subjects upon which no difference of opinion exists and so may be appreciated by all. "Job Charnock of the Mid-Day Halt" is perhaps the most attractive of the many spirited poems included in the book. In another vein is "Jute" a diverting parody of "Scots Wha Hae." We are promised a further selection of "Dâk's" verses which will be looked forward to with interest by readers who have derived pleasure from the present volume.

The Times (Literary Supplement), 14th January 1911.—Mr. Corfield, an auditor by profession, and a distinguished philatelist, is well known both in Birmingham and Calcutta as a clever writer for the press; and he collects here many of his effective Topical verses written in Calcutta in 1907-1910 about his pseudonym of "Dâk."